SpringerBriefs in Religious Studies

Springer Briefs in Religious Studies Series is designed to accommodate the growing social scientific research on religion focusing on contemporary issues derived from the challenges of religious diversity, globalization, ethics, law and politics, culture, history, philosophy, education, psychology, society issues, etc. The Series fulfills a scholarly demand for short publications focused on the discussion of new ideas, fieldwork experiences, challenging views, and methodological and theoretical approaches to religion, from a global perspective. The Series will publish innovative social scientific monographs and collections, through a high standard of ethnographic and sociological analysis, which combine scholarly rigor with readable prose for the benefit of scholars and students in various academic fields related to the world of religion. All books to be published in this Series will be fully peer-reviewed before final acceptance.

More information about this series at http://www.springer.com/series/13200

Tuula Sakaranaho · Timo Aarrevaara ·
Johanna Konttori
Editors

The Challenges of Religious Literacy

The Case of Finland

 Springer

Editors
Tuula Sakaranaho (iD)
University of Helsinki
Helsinki, Finland

Timo Aarrevaara
University of Lapland
Rovaniemi, Finland

Johanna Konttori (iD)
University of Helsinki
Helsinki, Finland

ISSN 2510-5035   ISSN 2510-5043   (electronic)
SpringerBriefs in Religious Studies
ISBN 978-3-030-47575-8   ISBN 978-3-030-47576-5   (eBook)
https://doi.org/10.1007/978-3-030-47576-5

This Springer imprint is published by the registered company Springer Nature Switzerland AG
The registered company address is: Gewerbestrasse 11, 6330 Cham, Switzerland

Acknowledgments

We wish to thank the Finnish Cultural Foundation for the financial support that enabled the open access publishing of this volume.

Contents

Notes on Contributors

Timo Aarrevaara is a Professor of Public Management at the University of Lapland, Principal investigator of the research team of Professions in Arctic Societies, Co-Editor in Spring Changing Academy Series, and has conducted number of scholarly projects.

Mulki Al-Sharmani is Associate Professor of Islamic and Middle Eastern Studies at the University of Helsinki. Her research combines lived and textual Islam. She researches and writes on Muslim family laws and family practices in Egypt and Finland; Somali modern diasporas; mosques and family well-being; Quranic ethics and hermeneutics; and the question of gender in Islamic interpretive tradition.

Johanna Konttori, Ph.D., is a Research Coordinator at the University of Helsinki. In her doctoral work (2015), she examined the political debates on headscarves and full veils in twenty-first-century France. Her main areas of expertise include state–religion relations, religions in the public sphere, and Islam, all in the European context. These topics also informed her postdoctoral research, in which she examined religious literacy in Finland.

Aini Linjakumpu is a University Lecturer in Politics at the Faculty of Sciences at the University of Lapland and Adjunct Professor at the Tampere University, Finland. Her research has focused on the political dimensions of religions in the context of Islam and the Christian religious movements and denominations, especially the Conservative Laestadianism, Jehovah's Witnesses, Pentecostal communities, and Old Order Amish. Theoretically, her research interests are related, among others, to communities, violence, network politics, and politics of emotions.

Tarja Mankkinen is a Master of Political Science, Head of Development, Ministry of the Interior, Police Department. She coordinates the prevention of violent extremism and radicalization in Finland and she is responsible for the National action plan for the prevention of violent radicalisation and extremism, adopted by the government in 2012, 2016, and 2019. She represents Finland in several EU task forces such as Steering Board on Radicalization and other international forums. She is also responsible for the cooperation with minority groups including religious minorities.

Sanna Mustasaari, Ph.D., is a postdoctoral researcher at the Faculty of Law, the University of Helsinki. She studies the legal regulation of families in different legal fields as well as intersections of law and religion. Her dissertation Rethinking recognition: Transnational families and belonging in law (2017) examined the recognition of transnational family ties.

Tapio Nykänen is an Adjunct Professor and University Lecturer in Political Science at the University of Lapland, Finland. His research interests include religion and politics, politics of indigeneity, identity politics, and politics of nature relations. As a researcher of religion, he has specialized in the Lutheran revival movement Laestadianism. He has studied especially politics associated with the movements' biggest branch, conservative Laestadianism, and Laestadianism in Sami cultures.

Teemu Pauha, Ph.D., is a psychologist and religion scholar at the University of Helsinki. He specializes in the social psychological study of religious identity and interreligious relations, primarily in the context of Islam in Europe. His current project focuses on the ways in which young Shia Muslims in Finland use the Quran in negotiations of identity and authority.

Inkeri Rissanen, Ph.D., is University Lecturer at the Faculty of Education and Culture, Tampere University. Her research interests include multicultural education, religions, and worldviews in education and Islamic religious education. Much of her research has focused on the inclusion of Muslims in public education. Currently, she is the principal investigator of Implicit theories of malleability as the core of teachers' intercultural competence (CORE) (2019-2022).

Tuula Sakaranaho, Ph.D., is Professor of the Study of Religions and Vice Dean, at the Faculty of Theology, the University of Helsinki. Her research interests concern the governance of religious diversity in a multicultural European society, with a special focus on religious freedom and Muslims in Europe. She has also published on religious education in Finland and on Islamic religious education in Finland and Ireland.

Marja Tiilikainen, Ph.D., is Senior Researcher at the Migration Institute of Finland. Her research has focused on issues such as Muslim minorities; everyday lived religion; cultural dimensions of health, illness, and healing; everyday security; and transnational family life. In particular, she has studied Somali diasporic communities and conducted ethnographic research in Finland, Canada, and Somalia.

Martin Ubani, Ph.d., MTheol, holds the chair of Professor of Religious Education at the School of Theology and the School of Educational Applied Science and Teacher Education at the University of Eastern Finland. His research interests include religion, multiculturalism and education, RE teacher education, and didactics of RE. He holds several Academic positions of trust. Since 2017, he has been a library fellow at the Van Leer Institute, Jerusalem.

Introduction: Setting the Stage

Tuula Sakaranaho, Timo Aarrevaara, and Johanna Konttori

Abstract Religion has become a pressing matter in different fields of multicultural European society, which raises the question as to how best to govern religious diversity. What we argue in this book is that a successful governance of religious diversity necessitates the development of religious literacy. As such, religious literacy can be understood in a variety of ways depending on the particular context. This book draws on different empirical case studies concerning Finland, covering traditional Finnish religious movements and issues pertaining to immigration and the growing ethnic and religious diversity of Finnish society. In doing so, it delves, among other matters, into the field of school education and state policies against radicalization and violence.

Keywords Religious literacy · Diversity · Governance · Finland

1 Pitfalls of Religious Illiteracy

In contemporary European society, approaches towards religion in the public sphere tend to be very contradictory. In the 1960s, many sociologists envisaged that the process of secularization would result in religion becoming obsolete in the European public sphere and hence relegated solely to the private sphere of personal belief and practice. This has not happened, however. For instance, religion is regularly in the headlines of world politics and security issues. In particular, social media has become a medium for personal opinions and even a platform for hate talk, in which religion is seen as a root cause of social problems faced by a multicultural European society. At the same time, the importance of religion in the public sphere is not necessarily recognized, or it is avoided as an awkward subject, due to the idea that religion does not concern the secular world. In the latter case, religion is seen as a matter best left

T. Sakaranaho (✉) · J. Konttori
University of Helsinki, Helsinki, Finland
e-mail: tuula.sakaranaho@helsinki.fi

T. Aarrevaara
University of Lapland, Rovaniemi, Finland

© The Author(s) 2020
T. Sakaranaho et al. (eds.), *The Challenges of Religious Literacy*,
SpringerBriefs in Religious Studies, https://doi.org/10.1007/978-3-030-47576-5_1

aside in the work of administrators and in the health and service sectors. In practice, the price paid for this line of thought is the spread of religious illiteracy.

In our view, religion is a pressing matter in all fields of a plural society. This raises the question of how best to govern religious diversity. What we argue in this book is that a successful governance of religious diversity requires the development of religious literacy. Only by the development of religious literacy is it possible to avoid the two main pitfalls that religious illiteracy may produce. On the one hand, religious illiteracy is obvious in cases where issues pertaining to religion are not recognized. In Finland, this may concern the members of traditional revivalist movements or new immigrant communities who follow certain rules arising from their religious convictions, especially in relation to sexuality and family. On the other, religious illiteracy may be apparent in converse cases where religion is taken as the main explanatory factor when dealing with certain ethnic and religious groups. Islam, in particular, is a religion that tends to attract stereotypes which gloss over other personal factors, including age, class, race, gender, and cultural differences. To put it simply, not all Muslims are religious or wish to be treated as such. Both of the aforementioned pitfalls can be avoided through the ability to understand and encounter religious diversity in a constructive manner. This kind of proficiency lies at the heart of religious literacy.

2 Approaching Religious Literacy

In recent decades, the metaphor of "literacy" has become very popular when describing the aims of a culturally sensitive education or social services (cultural literacy) or as the ability to critically approach the media, especially social media (media literacy). In a similar fashion, we utilize the metaphor of religious literacy in order to emphasize the need for sensitivity to religion, which as a very complex matter can take many forms and play many roles in contemporary society. As such, religious literacy is a contested concept and can be understood in a variety of ways. (See Biesta et al. 2019.) Because it is also context-specific, it has been suggested that what is actually needed is religious literacies (Davie and Dinham 2019, 25–26).

Research on religious literacy has its roots in the Anglo-American world. The concept has gained momentum notably through the work of Stephen Prothero (e.g. Prothero 2007), Diane L. Moore (e.g. Moore 2015), and Adam Dinham (with his colleagues) (e.g. Dinham et al. 2009; Dinham 2015b). There are different broad views on religious literacy, among them theological, sociological, and culturalist approaches (see Dinham and Jones 2010; Kähkönen 2016). To offer some definitions for religious literacy to start with, we mention the following.

Dinham and Jones (2010, 6) have collected points of consensus among the different approaches:

> We suggest that religious literacy lies, then, in having the knowledge and skills to recognise religious faith as a legitimate and important area for public attention, a degree of general

knowledge about at least some religious traditions, and an awareness of and ability to find out about others.

Its purpose is to avoid stereotypes, respect and learn from others, and build good relations across difference. In this it is a civic endeavour rather than a theological or religious one, and seeks to support a strong, cohesive, multi-faith society, which is inclusive of people from all faith traditions and none in a context that is largely suspicious and anxious about religion and belief.

Diane L. Moore's definition, adopted by the American Academy of Religion, is specifically targeted at educators and aims at fostering understanding of religions. According to Moore (2015, 30–31),

Religious literacy entails the ability to discern and analyze the fundamental intersections of religion and social/political/cultural life through multiple lenses. Specifically, a religiously literate person will possess 1) a basic understanding of the history, central texts (where applicable), beliefs, practices and contemporary manifestations of several of the world's religious traditions as they arose out of and continue to be shaped by particular social, historical and cultural contexts; and 2) the ability to discern and explore the religious dimensions of political, social and cultural expressions across time and place.

Religious literacy has often been studied in the context of education (e.g. Conroy 2015; Moore 2014; Dinham et al. 2017; Biesta et al. 2019) but also in relation to the media (Lövheim 2012), welfare (Dinham 2015a), radicalization, and extremism (Francis et al. 2015), law (Melloni and Cadeddu 2019), political discourse (Konttori 2019), and NGOs (Siirto and Hammar 2016). In this book we approach religious literacy in different contexts, such as city politics, mosque associations, and state administration. The chapters are connected to the research project on religious literacy, funded by the Finnish Cultural Foundation (2019–2020).

In *Religious Literacy in Policy and Practice*, Dinham and Francis (2015, 3) summarize religious literacy, first, as a matter of general interest and, second, as something that is specific to a particular context. The book at hand combines these two approaches in order to highlight the importance of religious literacy in a pluralizing and secularizing European society while utilizing empirical cases concerning religious literacy in the national context of Finland. However, it does not treat religious literacy as taken for granted but rather as needing to be problematized as a general concept used when referring to religion and religious diversity in European society.

In a similar fashion as many other European countries, Finland has undergone rapid social change invariably linked with processes of secularization and globalization. On the one hand, Finnish society is very secular, and hence religion does not dictate what people believe or how they behave. At the same time, partly due to immigration, there is an urgent need to come to terms with growing social, cultural, and religious diversity, as well as to develop social policies that address specific issues linked with different religious traditions and arising from this diversity. (See Sorsa 2018; Illman et al. 2017; Ketola et al. 2011.) It is obvious that some sort of discrepancy exists between these two forces. Due to the process of secularization, people's knowledge and understanding of religion are diminishing at the very moment when it would be most needed. One answer to this problem is to develop general religious literacy (see Davie 2015).

We fully agree with Dinham and Francis that data and new theories are needed in order to complement or alter the perceptions of religion in religious education in school or in the study of religions at the university level (see also Nash and Bishop 2010; Biesta et al. 2019). Even more so, a new understanding is needed with respect to popular and media portrayals of religion, or in relation to public discussion about religion. However, we are somewhat critical of the view that, with the help of religious literacy, one could "reveal a *real* religious landscape", as argued by Dinham and Francis (2015, 3, italics ours). The epistemological starting point of this volume lies in social constructivism, on the basis of which we approach religious literacy as a conceptual lens that, when put into practice, can produce different versions of a religious landscape.

In Finnish society, there are many situations where there is a grave lack of mutual trust and understanding between different parties (for instance, the administration and industry). For decades, Finland was understood to be a nation that shares common values. The increase of multicultural and secular features of Finnish society has somewhat changed the situation. In order to come to terms with the complexities of a diversifying and secularizing society, it is necessary to look at religious literacy from the perspective of multi-level governance, where a state-centred analysis is broadened to the processes of decentralization of traditional administrative functions and hence to civil society, businesses or international organizations, such as the European Union. By utilizing the approach of multi-level governance, in addition to focusing on formal organizations one can also examine networks and financial instruments related to policy programs or international agreements. Moreover, multi-level governance makes it possible to take into account how cultures and religions can function as a resource and as a means of co-cooperation in the public sphere. Being a strength of society, multiculturalism enables the use of versatile governance tools. (See Martikainen 2013.)

The aim of this book is to add to the capacity for better governance, decision-making, and societal interaction. We are looking for ways in which religious literacy can make available operational resources for actors in multi-level governance. This knowledge is essential for religious communities, working life, public decision-making, and public-funded service structures. We also aim to encourage readers to find solutions based on religious literacy that go beyond traditional conflicts. The chapters of this book present new ways of working with religious communities, public authorities, and citizens by using deliberative methods to find sustainable solutions.

3 Summary of the Chapters

This book consists of seven chapters in total. Following the introduction, five thematic chapters investigate religious literacy in relation to both majority and minority religions in Finland: the Evangelical Lutheran Church, Islam, and Conservative Laestadianism. What ties these chapters together is their common aim towards understanding the forms of religious literacy, as well as religious illiteracy, present in different contexts and communities in Finnish society.

Teemu Pauha and Johanna Konttori investigate statements made by candidates in the Helsinki City Council election in 2017 regarding the plan to build "a grand mosque" in Helsinki. They ask how Islam in general and the mosque project in particular are represented in the data. In the statements, what are the blind spots regarding religion? In what ways is religion misunderstood or even misrepresented? In their analysis, Pauha and Konttori identify the main discourses, or ways of representing, Islam and the mosque project, including the strong emphasis put on the freedom of religion in general. These discourses present Islam, and the mosque project in particular, as somewhat challenging to the freedom of religion, reflecting problems that could come along with the building of the mosque, as well as vis-à-vis Islam as a religion, in relation to foreignness. The authors argue that even in a secular country, politicians need to have knowledge about religions in order to be able to make fact-based decisions regarding issues related to them and religious communities.

Tapio Nykänen and Aini Linjakumpu focus on Conservative Laestadianism, which is the biggest revival movement inside the Finnish Lutheran Church and the largest Christian revival movement in Scandinavia. In their chapter, they scrutinize the regional and municipal political role of Conservative Laestadianism in the northern parts of the Finnish "Bible Belt", where the movement has prominent support, and they also examine the business networks of Conservative Laestadians. The authors aim to understand what features of politics and business exercised by Laestadians or associated with them should be recognized or understood as "Laestadian". Moreover, they ask, what does it mean for regional public life if the religion has an effect on the actions of Laestadian politicians and entrepreneurs? Do politics and business in the core regions of the movement become "Laestadianized"? In other words, how strong is the sociopolitical and financial influence of Conservative Laestadianism in the regions where the movement has strong support?

Inkeri Rissanen, Martin Ubani and Tuula Sakaranaho focus on three particular manifestations of religious illiteracy, and they analyse how these influence the governance of religious diversity in Finnish multi-faith schools. These three manifestations of religious illiteracy, which have emerged in their previous case studies, are: (1) simplified ways of making distinctions between religion and culture, (2) an inability to recognize and handle intra-religious diversity, and (3) naturalization of the Protestant conceptions of religion, culture, and citizenship. A theme that runs across these aspects of religious illiteracy is how they reflect the tendencies of either religionization or "religion-blindness". To conclude, the chapter reflects on the question of how to develop the governance of religious diversity in Finnish schools so that the pitfalls of religious illiteracy can be avoided.

Mulki Al-Sharmani and Sanna Mustasaari draw on past research (conducted separately by each of the authors) and ongoing joint research on the processes through which Muslims in Finland secure divorces, both Islamic and civil. The authors focus on how Finnish Muslims of Somali background draw on norms of both state law and Islamic law in their divorce practices in a non-binary way. They also examine how certain selected Helsinki mosques understand Islamic divorce in relation to court-issued civil divorce, and how they see their role and authority vis-à-vis that of state institutions in the processes of arbitrating divorce disputes and issuing Islamic divorces. The analysis problematizes three central points. The first is the assumed homogeneity and fixedness of what is "religious" about the divorce processes and how the concept of religious literacy can advance understanding of Islamic family law with regard to women's agency. The second point is the assumed oppositional relationship between "secular" and "religious" (read Islamic) divorce reflected in state laws and discourses, as well as in Muslim divorce practices. The last point concerns the insufficient attention to the importance of gender and impact of mosque mediation and arbitration in family disputes, particularly in relation to women's agency.

Marja Tiilikainen and Tarja Mankkinen discuss in their chapter how the authorities in Finland have juggled, on one hand, the need to build good and trusted relationships with Muslim communities and to support the creation of a tolerant multicultural society, and on the other hand, the need to prevent violent radicalization and extremism in Finland without stigmatizing Muslim communities. The authors understand religious literacy as a kind of sensitivity among the authorities to religion and religious communities. Empirically, the chapter is based on analysis of two national action plans for the prevention of violent extremism, as well as Mankkinen's long-term experience with security-related issues at the Ministry of the Interior.

The book ends with a conclusion that brings together the different contexts of religious (il)literacy discussed in the previous chapters and then looks at their similarities and differences. Also considered is the impact of the book on academic research and beyond.

References

Biesta, G., Aldrige, D., Hannam, P., & Whittle, S. (2019). *Religious literacy: A way forward for religious education? A report submitted to the Culham St Gabriel's Trust.* Brunel University London & Hampshire Inspection and Advisory Services. Retrieved November 27, 2019, from https://www.reonline.org.uk/wp-content/uploads/2019/07/Religious-Literacy-Biesta-Aldridge-Hannam-Whittle-June-2019.pdf.
Conroy, J. C. (2015). Religious illiteracy in school religious education. In A. Dinham & M. Francis (Eds.), *Religious literacy in policy and practice* (pp. 167–185). Bristol: Policy Press.
Davie, G. (2015). Foreword. In A. Dinham & M. Francis (Eds.), *Religious literacy in policy and practice* (pp. vii–xi). Bristol: Policy Press.
Davie, G., & Dinham, A. (2019). Religious literacy in modern Europe. In A. Melloni & F. Cadeddu (Eds.), *Religious literacy, law and history: perspectives on European pluralist societies* (pp. 17–28). London: Routledge.
Dinham, A. (2015a). Religious literacy and welfare. In A. Dinham & M. Francis (Eds.), *Religious literacy in policy and practice* (pp. 101–111). Bristol: Policy Press.

Dinham, A. (2015b). Grace Davie and religious literacy: Undoing a lamentable quality of conversation. In A. Day & M. Lövheim (Eds.), *Modernities, memory and mutations: Grace Davie and the study of religion* (pp. 45–58). Farnham: Ashgate.

Dinham, A., & Francis, M. (Eds.). (2015). *Religious literacy in policy and practice*. Bristol: Policy Press.

Dinham, A., Francis, M., & Shaw, M. (2017). Towards a theory and practice of religious literacy: A case study of religion and belief engagement in a UK university. *Religions, 8*(12), 276.

Dinham, A., Furbey, R., & Lowndes, V. (Eds.). (2009). *Faith in the public realm: Controversies, policies and practices*. Bristol: Policy Press.

Dinham, A., & Jones, S. H. (2010). *Religious literacy leadership in higher education: an analysis of key issues and challenges for university leaders*. Report. Religious Literacy Leadership in Higher Education Programme, York. Retrieved December 16, 2019, from http://research.gold.ac.uk/id/eprint/3916.

Francis, M., van Eck, A., & van Twist, D. (2015). Religious literacy, radicalisation and extremism. In A. Dinham & M. Francis (Eds.), *Religious literacy in policy and practice* (pp. 113–134). Bristol: Policy Press.

Illman, R., Ketola, K., Latvio, R., & Sohlberg, J. (Eds.). (2017). *Monien uskontojen ja katsomusten Suomi*. Kirkon tutkimuskeskuksen verkkojulkaisuja 48. Retrieved December 16, 2019, from https://evl.fi/documents/1327140/45386794/Ktk+-+Monien+uskontojen+ja+katsom usten+Suomi/c8c8d8be-e49b-5998-3539-6b2a29a4903d.

Ketola, K., Niemelä, K., Palmu, H., & Salomäki, H. (2011). *Uskonto suomalaisten elämässä. Uskonnollinen kasvatus, moraali, onnellisuus ja suvaitsevaisuus kansainvälisessä vertailussa.* Yhteiskuntatieteellisen tietoarkiston julkaisuja 9. Tampere: Yhteiskuntatieteellinen tietoarkisto, Tampereen yliopisto.

Konttori, J. (2019). Uskontolukutaito tutkimuksen kohteena. Diskursiivinen näkökulma. *Uskonnontutkija-Religionsforskaren* 8, 1. https://doi.org/10.24291/uskonnontutkija.v8i1.83248.

Kähkönen, E. (2016). Uskontolukutaito sekulaarin ja uskonnollisen välisenä siltana. In R. Gothóni, S. Hyväri, M. Kolkka, & P. Vuokila-Oikkonen (Eds.), *Osallisuus yhteiskunnallisena haasteena: Diakonia-ammattikorkeakoulun TKI-toiminnan vuosikirja 2* (pp. 261–274). Diak Työelämä, 7. Helsinki: Diakonia-ammattikorkeakoulu. Retrieved December 16, 2019, from http://urn.fi/URN: ISBN:978-952-493-275-2.

Lövheim, M. (2012). Religious socialization in a media age. *Nordic Journal of Religion and Society, 25*(2), 151–168.

Martikainen, T. (2013). Multilevel and pluricentric network governance of religion. In T. Martikainen, & F. Gauthier (Eds.), *Religion in the neoliberal age. Political economy and modes of governance* (pp. 129–142). Farnham: Ashgate.

Melloni, A., & Cadeddu, F. (Eds.). (2019). *Religious literacy, law and history: Perspectives on European pluralist societies.*, ICLARS series on law and religion London and New York: Routledge.

Moore, D. L. (2014). Overcoming religious illiteracy: Expanding the boundaries of religious education. *Religious Education, 109*(4), 379–389.

Moore, D. L. (2015). Diminishing religious literacy: Methodological assumptions and analytical frameworks for promoting the public understanding of religion. In A. Dinham & M. Francis (Eds.), *Religious literacy in policy and practice* (pp. 27–38). Bristol: Policy Press.

Nash, R. J., & Bishop, P. A. (2010). *Teaching adolescents religious literacy in a Post-9/11 World.* Charlotte, NC: Information Age Publishing.

Prothero, S. (2007). *Religious literacy: What every American needs to know–and doesn't.* San Francisco: HarperSanFrancisco.

Siirto, U., & Hammar, S. (2016). Kansalaisjärjestöt moniuskontoisen ympäristön toimijoina ja uskontolukutaidon edistäjinä. In P.-L. Rauhala, M. Jäppinen, A. Metteri, & S. Ranta-Tyrkkö (Eds.), *Kansainvälinen, ylirajainen, globaali sosiaalityö–juuria, katkoksia, uusia alkuja* (pp. 178–203). Sosiaalityön tutkimuksen vuosikirja. Tallinn: United Press Global.

Sorsa, L. (2018). *Uskonnolliset tavat ja julkinen tila Suomessa.* Kirkon tutkimuskeskuksen verkkojulkaisuja 55. Retrieved December 16, 2019, from https://evl.fi/documents/1327140/409 00428/Ktk+-+uskonnolliset+tavat+ja+julkinen+tila+Suomessa/5067ac74-bf93-2619-d695-80a 81dfd22b3.

"There Is Freedom of Religion in Finland, But…" The Helsinki Mosque Debate

Teemu Pauha and Johanna Konttori

Abstract In this chapter, we examine statements of Finnish municipal election candidates regarding plans to build a "grand mosque" and cultural centre in central Helsinki. Despite proclaiming support for the universal freedom of religion, the candidates were hesitant to apply it to the mosque case. Opponents of the mosque project emphasized the Christian heritage of Finland and portrayed the proposed mosque as a channel through which foreign conflicts could enter Finnish society. The mosque was also opposed because it was seen as a "political" project instead of a "religious" one. The proponents of the mosque, in turn, considered it to be a "Muslim church" and therefore entitled to the same treatment as Christian houses of worship. The mosque was also seen as important to the local Muslim community, but very few candidates considered the possibility of the mosque (or Islam) making a positive contribution to the broader society. Besides identifying the key discourses, we reflect on them from a religious literacy perspective.

Keywords Finland · Helsinki · Religious literacy · Discourse · Election · Islam · Mosque

1 Introduction

The sociologist of religion Grace Davie has written about the factors that should be taken into account when talking about religion in present-day Europe. These factors include, among others, the role that Christianity has played—and still plays—in European societies, immigration to Europe from different parts of the world (which has shaped—and still shapes—the religious field of the continent), and the growing realization that regarding religions and religiosity, Europe is not the model that the rest of the world follows. In particular, Muslims challenge the traditional ideas, models and customs of Europe, even by their mere presence. (Davie and Dinham 2019, 17–22.)

T. Pauha (✉) · J. Konttori
University of Helsinki, Helsinki, Finland
e-mail: teemu.pauha@helsinki.fi

© The Author(s) 2020
T. Sakaranaho et al. (eds.), *The Challenges of Religious Literacy*,
SpringerBriefs in Religious Studies, https://doi.org/10.1007/978-3-030-47576-5_2

9

The number of Muslims in Western Europe has grown rapidly since the Second World War, and in many European countries Islam is now the second largest religion. This change has sparked many political discussions and debates, many of which have dealt with visible signs of Islamic faith in the predominantly Christian/secular European landscape. Two aspects in particular have aroused suspicions and opposition: the use of hijabs and niqabs (Nilsson 2018; Konttori 2015; Brems 2014) and the building and financing of mosques, including the training of the imams working there (Hashas et al. 2018; Allievi 2009; Cesari 2005).

The discussions and debates concerning Islam and Muslims have varied in their intensity from country to country, but nevertheless they exist in most Western European countries in one form or another. Finland is no exception. While a small Tatar community has been living in the country for more than a century, and controversies and debates rarely concern them in any way, the majority of Muslims in Finland who immigrated from the early 1990s onwards have received much more attention from the media, politicians and ordinary citizens. Questions concerning headscarves, niqabs, mosques, burial and butchery practices have been raised in Finland, but the discussions have remained relatively calm.

Currently there are only two purpose-built mosque buildings in Finland. These are situated in the small town of Järvenpää and in Helsinki, respectively, and belong to the Tatars. In January 2015, a conglomerate of two Muslim organisations and an interfaith dialogue group applied for land to build a "grand mosque" and cultural centre in central Helsinki. The conglomerate wanted to keep the mosque independent of existing Muslim associations, and therefore it created a separate foundation named Oasis to manage its affairs. (Pauha and Konttori 2019.) The Helsinki mosque project was debated for several years, receiving a great deal of attention, at least in the capital region.

One of the main issues during the mosque debate concerned foreign funding. The organizers of the mosque project had negotiated with Bahrain, and there were fears that with outside money there would also come foreign influence in relation to the type of Islam practised in Finland. In addition, the estimated building costs of the mosque were quite high, totalling over 100 million Euros, and the maintenance costs would also have been considerable. These aspects led to astonishment and drew criticism. Another issue was the representativeness of the mosque. It was supposed to be open to all Muslims, but doubts arose whether in practice the Shi'a would be included. Furthermore, not all Muslim communities active in Helsinki were supportive of the project. (Pauha and Konttori 2019; see also Pauha and Martikainen 2017.)

In December 2017, the Urban Environment Division of the City of Helsinki proposed that the Urban Environment committee accept the application and reserve a plot for the mosque complex, albeit with conditions. Despite this, the committee unanimously rejected the application in a meeting held the very next week. The committee concluded that the application was untenable because "the scope of the project and the still open questions and uncertainty factors, above all the origin of the funding and the possible effects of the funding sources, do not provide a sustainable foundation for this solution to be realized." The mosque plan was scheduled to be further discussed by the City Board of Helsinki, but after it was rejected by the Urban

Environment committee, the applicants decided to withdraw the application. (Pauha and Konttori 2019.)

In this chapter, we investigate comments made by electoral candidates in the Helsinki City Council election in Spring 2017 and study how they argued either for or against the mosque plan. The data consists of the responses given by the candidates to a specific statement presented by the leading daily newspaper in Finland, the *Helsingin Sanomat*: "It is possible to build a grand mosque for Helsinki if no city or state money is spent on the project." The candidates were asked to rate on a scale of 1–5 whether they agreed with the statement or not, with 1 meaning "totally disagree", 3 meaning "don't know", and 5 meaning "totally agree". Altogether 848 candidates gave their rating. The distribution of responses is shown in Table 1.

As can be seen in the last row of Table 1, approximately one third of the candidates were at least somewhat opposed to the mosque project, while little over half were in favour of it. Opposition to the mosque was strongest among the candidates of the populist-nationalist Finns Party, centre-right National Coalition Party, Independence Party (known for being Eurosceptic), and Christian Democrats, while the candidates of all other parties were generally in favour of the project.

Besides giving numerical ratings, the candidates could justify their answers by writing open responses. Altogether 630 out of 848 respondents chose to do so. In the rest of this chapter, we focus on those 630 responses. We have coded their contents in a bottom-up manner, that is, without a pre-existing coding scheme, using the following questions as guidance: How are Islam in general and the mosque project in particular represented in the data? How do the candidates understand religion and its role in society? What are the blind spots regarding religion in their statements?

We identified several key discourses—ways of representing the issue at hand— that underlie the responses. In the following we take a closer look at these discourses, pointing out the main lines of argumentation as well as the rhetorical choices made to strengthen the candidates' arguments. In order to exemplify each discourse we present several illustrative quotes from the data.

We reflect on the discourses from a religious literacy perspective. We understand religious literacy in the vein of Moore (2007, p. 56) as "the ability to discern and analyze the fundamental intersections of religion and social/political/cultural life through multiple lenses". We have chosen Moore's approach to religious literacy because of the emphasis that it places on complex interconnections between religious and other aspects of social reality. As will be seen in the following pages, religion is often perceived as problematic insofar as it intertwines with politics. This is especially the case with Islam; in public discussion, Islam is regularly portrayed as something inextricably political, even to the extent of being "politics in religious disguise". Accordingly, many of the responses analysed here argue that religion and politics need to be kept separate, or otherwise they will taint each other. Moore (2007, 2015), however, thinks differently. For her, the intertwining of religion and politics is not a problem in itself. Rather, it is just the way things are. Religion is always to some extent political, and vice versa. Religious literacy is about discerning the subtle ways in which religion intersects with other fields of human activity.

Table 1 The distribution of responses (1 = "totally disagree", 3 = "don't know", 5 = "totally agree") given to the statement: "It is possible to build a grand mosque to Helsinki, if no city or state money is spent on the project."

Party	1	2	3	4	5	Total
Social Democratic Party	11 (9.6%)	19 (16.5%)	17 (14.8%)	51 (44.3%)	17 (14.8%)	115 (100.0%)
Centre Party	4 (5.4%)	13 (17.6%)	6 (8.1%)	30 (40.5%)	21 (28.4%)	74 (100.0%)
National Coalition Party	21 (18.9%)	48 (43.2%)	6 (5.4%)	29 (26.1%)	7 (6.3%)	111 (100.0%)
Swedish People's Party	1 (2.0%)	8 (16.3%)	5 (8.2%)	29 (59.2%)	7 (14.3%)	49 (100.0%)
Christian Democrats	39 (54.9%)	15 (21.1%)	6 (8.5%)	9 (12.7%)	2 (2.8%)	71 (100.0%)
Green League	1 (0.8%)	9 (7.3%)	13 (10.6%)	65 (52.8%)	35 (28.5%)	123 (100.0%)
Left Alliance	5 (4.8%)	9 (8.6%)	10 (9.5%)	56 (53.3%)	25 (23.8%)	105 (100.0%)
Finns Party	62 (72.1%)	10 (11.6%)	3 (3.5%)	7 (8.1%)	4 (4.7%)	86 (100.0%)
Communist Party	3 (8.1%)	4 (10.8%)	2 (5.4%)	15 (40.5%)	13 (35.1%)	37 (100.0%)
Liberal Party	0 (0.0%)	3 (20.0%)	2 (13.3%)	5 (33.3%)	5 (33.3%)	15 (100.0%)
Pirate Party	2 (8.3%)	2 (8.3%)	1 (4.2%)	7 (29.2%)	12 (50.0%)	24 (100.0%)
Feminist Party	1 (4.3%)	6 (26.1%)	0 (0.0%)	14 (60.9%)	2 (8.7%)	23 (100.0%)
Independence Party	4 (57.1%)	1 (14.3%)	1 (14.3%)	1 (14.3%)	0 (0.0%)	7 (100.0%)
Other[a]	2 (25.0%)	1 (12.5%)	0 (0.0%)	3 (37.5%)	2 (25.0%)	8 (100.0%)
Total	156 (18.4%)	148 (17.5%)	71 (8.4%)	321 (37.9%)	152 (17.9%)	848 (100.0%)

[a]The "Other" category includes independent candidates and parties with three or fewer candidates (e.g. the Animal Justice Party and Communist Workers' Party)

Moore (2015) advocates a cultural studies approach as an antidote to diminishing religious literacy. According to her, such an approach entails, for example, three central claims with regard to religion: first, religions are not monolithic but internally diverse; secondly, religions are not static but evolving and changing; and lastly, religions do not function in an isolated "religious" sphere but influence all aspects of culture. As we will demonstrate in the following pages, these three claims can provide a valuable corrective to the blind spots demonstrated by the comments of the electoral candidates.

We argue that even in a secular country, politicians need to have knowledge about religions in order to be able to make fact-based decisions on issues related to religions and religious communities. Questions regarding religious literacy do not concern only Islam, but they still often have something to do with it, especially in contemporary Western Europe, where the number of Muslims and the significance of Islam have grown rapidly.

2 Domestic Christianity, Foreign Islam

The first hegemonic discourse that we identified in our data constructs a juxtaposition between Christianity and Islam, with the former as something Finnish while the latter is not. Several of the responses mentioned conflicts that would supposedly be caused by the mosque. These conflicts were typically portrayed as imported from abroad. The general idea appeared to be that foreign funding would be accompanied by a radical agenda that in some unspecified way might permeate into the Finnish Muslim community. The idea that radicalism could develop inside the Finnish Muslim community without foreign involvement was not taken into account. Both of these ideas held religious ideologies and communities to be static: if the foreign funder had some sort of an agenda, it would simply be transferred to Finland, and Muslims in the country would accept it without any critical thinking.

> On the other hand, the transfer of the conservative thoughts of the foreign funders to the Finnish Muslim population causes threatening visions. (Male, Liberal Party, 4)[1]

> No Saudi money for Helsinki. It does not come free of charge. Elsewhere radicalization has been significant in mosques funded by Saudi Arabia. (Male, Finns Party, 1)

In the latter statement, it is noted (with no further specification) that funding of a mosque by Saudi Arabia has led to radicalization "elsewhere". This is one of the many examples of how the Helsinki mosque debate was transnational by nature. Several respondents referred to experiences in other countries, and thus the debate was never only about Helsinki and Finland. Quite obviously, this also has a lot to do with the fact that the funding of the mosque was coming from abroad. The transnational aspect of the debate will be discussed further on.

Another thing to note is the vagueness of the statement. The respondent does not give any indication of which countries or mosques he is referring to. The statement gives the impression that the respondent has studied the issue, as he is referring to previous mosque projects, but the vagueness actually takes a lot of credibility away. While it is true that foreign funding and influence over European Muslims has had effects in the European context (see, e.g., Rohe 2019), it would be too

---

[1] The number in parentheses refers to the numerical rating (1 = "totally disagree", 3 = "don't know", 5 = "totally agree") given to the statement: "It is possible to build a grand mosque to Helsinki, if no city or state money is spent on the project."

much to claim that all of the Saudi-funded mosques in Europe are extremist or radical actors (Inge 2016, 28–29). The word "elsewhere" in the statement gives the impression that Saudi funding and radicalization go hand in hand. Also, and quite interestingly, in statements which bring up the threat of radicalization in Finland there is no specification of who would bring that radicalization. One possible actor could be imams. Whether imams should be trained in Europe or, for example, in Saudi Arabia has been debated and investigated in many European countries (Hashas et al. 2018), Finland included (Martikainen and Latvio 2018). It is somewhat surprising that imams were only rarely mentioned in the data.

The fear of radicalization being brought from abroad is evident in the following statement as well:

> As far as we know, the funding would come from actors supportive of the ultraconservative Salafi branch of Islam, which might further the spread of radical thought in Finland. (Male, Liberal Party, 2)

Why was radicalization perceived solely as a threat from abroad? Arguably, this may demonstrate the extent to which popular conceptions of Islam are based on media coverage. Raittila and Maasilta (2008) have noted that when discussing Islam in other countries, Finnish newspapers have a strong tendency to associate it with terrorism and political violence. However, the same kind of association is not made in newspaper stories that are about Islam and Muslims in Finland. When Finnish Muslims are described as being involved in conflicts, the conflicts are between Islamic religious practices and the Finnish legislation, and not violent in nature. (Raittila and Maasilta 2008.)

The statement above also mentions "the ultraconservative Salafi branch of Islam", linking it to "radical thought". As Inge (2016) has noted, Salafism is often assumed to be both a political and (potentially) violent movement, even though the opposite is often the truth. Here, religious illiteracy appears to manifest itself in the form of a lack of knowledge. Inge conducted her research on Salafi women in London and Birmingham, and she notes that all of the Salafi communities that she got to know during her fieldwork were categorically against both political action and violence. We cannot know for sure what the candidate of the Liberal Party meant by "radical thought", but at least some connection with either political or violent action can be assumed.

All in all, it remains unclear whether the candidates were primarily worried about violent extremism or anti-liberal values, because they associated the mosque project (with little elaboration) with both. However, as Moore (2015) has emphasized, religious literacy involves an awareness of the internal diversity of religious traditions. It is necessary, for example, to acknowledge the distinction between religious conservatism and religiously motivated violence. Conservative religious groups, both Islamic and otherwise, can be opposed to issues such as gender equality and democracy, without this translating into violent extremist action.

Besides the potential for conflicts associated with the mosque, Islam in general was often portrayed as foreign and Christianity as the religion of Finland. It appears that a large mosque was seen to be too dominant in the Christian environment and culture, according to the respondents.

> Finland is still a Christian country. (Female, Christian Democrats, 1)
>
> A grand mosque does not fit into the Finnish culture and our way of life. (Male, National Coalition Party, 1)
>
> Finland is a Christian country. It is not allowed to build large Christian churches in any Muslim country, and in many cases not any kind of Christian shrine is allowed. (Male, Social Democratic Party, 1)

The transnational nature of the debate is again visible in the statement in which it is pointed out that Christians are not allowed to build large churches in Muslim countries. This statement implicitly suggests that if Christians are not allowed to build churches in Muslim countries, then Muslims should not be allowed to build a grand mosque in a Christian country.

The idea of the foreignness of Islam was often conveyed implicitly by unquestioningly assuming that Muslims in Finland are immigrants. An example of this is the following excerpt, which refers to the "home country" of the Muslims. While it remains unclear what the country in question is, the choice of words shows that it is certainly not Finland.

> I do not think that the Shias and the Sunnis would be able to practise their religion in the same mosque, as they are not able to do that even in their home country. (Female, Christian Democrats, 1)

As demonstrated by the examples above, many of the respondents consider Finland to be a "Christian country" or "Christian state". This is in line with Davie's point, presented earlier, on the significance of Christian heritage in Europe. Coming from an election candidate, the notion of the Finnish state as "Christian" is problematic because, at least in the legal sense, it is untrue; despite granting special judicial status to the Evangelical Lutheran Church and Orthodox Church, Finland has no official religion, and the state is confessionally neutral (Kääriäinen 2011; Sorsa 2015). However, as discussed in Pauha (2018) and Pauha and Jasinskaja-Lahti (2013), the public representations of Finnishness are still very much intertwined with Christianity; this may maintain the idea of a homogeneously Christian state and, as a result, exclude religious minorities from perceptions of true Finnishness.

The notion of the Finnish state as "Christian" is especially noteworthy, as it comes from candidates wishing to represent the capital of Finland. As in many other European countries, (Muslim) immigrants to Finland tend to live in the biggest cities. Accordingly, Helsinki is probably the most multicultural city in Finland, and its inhabitants confess an array of different faiths. In this context, the emphasis put on a "Christian" Finland may represent an ideal held by a candidate, but it hardly reflects the multireligious reality in the city, in which approximately one half of the inhabitants are not members of the majority church (Helsingin seurakuntayhtymä 2018).

3 Contested Boundaries of Religion

A particularly prominent discourse concerned the freedom of religion and its limits. Regardless of party affiliation, candidates emphasized the necessity for religious freedom and the equal treatment of all religions by the state. In the very next instant, however, they often gave reasons for restricting these rights in the case of the Helsinki mosque project. Frequently used were statements in the vein of "there is freedom of religion in Finland, but…" Examples of this discourse include:

> In the name of freedom of religion, it is of course allowed to build shrines of different religions in Helsinki, but on the basis of existing knowledge, I do not support this project. (Male, Green League, 2)
>
> People of all religious denominations need to have their place in Helsinki for religious practice, but there have been bad experiences of grand mosques elsewhere in the world. (Female, National Coalition Party, 1)

In the statement above, the mosque debate is once again linked to previous experiences "elsewhere in the world", and thus the transnational aspect of the debate is brought up. And again, the statement includes a vague reference to somewhere else in the world. This vagueness makes it impossible for the voters, or researchers for that matter, to check the claim concerning bad experiences in relation to grand mosques. This is apparent in the following statement as well, where the respondent does not refer only to "bad experiences" but also to hate and terrorism. Again, it is impossible to know which cases the respondent is referring to. Positive examples from "elsewhere" are conspicuously absent. Religious literacy, as understood by Moore, would require that the heterogeneity of Muslim communities and their mosques receive attention. Here Islam and grand mosques are presented only in a problem-oriented manner.

> Every religion has the right to have a place where to worship their God. But mosques in other countries have been used to instigate hate and to support terrorism. (Male, Finns Party, 2)

The statements were often very general and abstract with regard to religious freedom. A few candidates even quoted directly from the European Convention on Human Rights or similar treaties. It is not far-fetched to interpret this as an electoral tactic: by making declarations in support of religious freedom, the election candidates could signal their commitment to general democratic values.

Upon close reading of the statements, it appears that many of the candidates were operating on the implicit assumption that true religion excludes politics. Accordingly, the mosque project was perceived as problematic because it was considered to be political instead of religious—or even political in religious disguise. Some examples include:

> The grand mosque is more of a political project than a possibility to practise religion. (Male, Left Alliance, 1)
>
> Islam is not a religion, but a conservative political ideology. (Female, Finns Party, 1)

As van der Veer (1996) has illustrated, the idea of true religion as antithetical to politics is the product of Western Enlightenment thought, which restricted the role of religion to the private sphere. True religion, as it is understood in the post-Enlightenment West, is about harmony and goodwill, whereas politics is about division and conflict (van der Veer 1996; see Pauha 2017). Similar views on religion are conveyed, for example, in the following excerpts:

> The core message of all true religions is the same, namely, the equality of and brotherly love among all people. However, the mosque that is planned for Helsinki would represent Wahhabism, disguised as Islam. (Male, Independence Party, 1)

> In this project religion and politics seem to intertwine, and that might put a strain on relations between Muslims representing different denominations. (Female, Green League, 4)

> It needs to be ensured that the rationally selected location is for practising one's religion, not for agitating people. (Male, Finns Party, 4)

That Islam is considered to be "political" instead of purely religious is a relatively widespread discourse in contemporary Europe. From a religious literacy perspective, however, such a strict demarcation between religion and other fields of human activity is questionable. Moore (2015, 31) emphasizes that religious literacy involves understanding religion "*in context* and as *inextricably woven into all dimensions of human experience*" (italics in the original). A religiously literate person is able to look past popular preconceptions about certain religious traditions or religion in general and perceive the complex interconnections between religion and other facets of human culture. In addition, the claim that the mosque "would represent Wahhabism, disguised as Islam", suggests that Wahhabism is not Islam. This is factually incorrect.

Furthermore, as scholars such as Taira (2010, 2013) have argued, religion is not a clearly bounded entity to be found in the social world but a classificatory device that can be applied to any number of things in order to advance goals related to them. With the status of religion come certain (both official and unofficial) privileges and burdens. The demarcation of religion is therefore inextricably tied to issues of power and dominance.

Definitions can be used as tools for the governance of religion. The choice of one definition over others may be used to legitimize religious restrictions without appearing to violate the freedom of religion. As we have discussed above, a number of electoral candidates emphasized their commitment to religious freedom while at the same time opposing the proposed mosque. Such a rhetorical move was easier, of course, if the mosque could be placed outside the boundaries of religion. The same strategy has also been used, for example, in political debates in France on headscarves and veils (Konttori 2015).

In contrast to those denying Islam the status of a religion, commentators with a favourable attitude towards the proposed mosque tended to perceive it as a straightforward equivalent of a Christian church. A few of the statements even used the term "church" in reference to a mosque.

> I see mosques, just like churches, as places for practising one's religion. (Male, Left Alliance, 5)

> We do, after all, have churches representing other denominations as well. (Male, Left Alliance, 4)

> If we have a grand church [referring to Helsinki Cathedral], then why not a grand mosque? (Male, Left Alliance, 4)

> It is possible to build a grand mosque, just like the churches of all other religions. (Female, National Coalition Party, 4)

One could question the term "Muslim church" by pointing out that, despite overlapping, the roles of a church and a mosque are not identical. Read in context, however, the choice of words here do not seem to imply a one-to-one correspondence between the functions of the two buildings, but a very general idea of both being houses of worship and therefore entitled to the same treatment.[2]

Besides perceiving the mosque as a "Muslim church", the favourable commentators tended to regard the activities of the mosque as internal affairs of the Muslim community. The mosque plan was welcomed because Muslims were thought to need it. A lack of space was perceived as the most pressing of their needs.

> In a situation where there is a lack of prayer rooms and suitable locations for practising religion, the grand mosque is an important project for the Muslim community. (Female, Left Alliance, 5)

Reading the statements, one gets an impression of the Finnish Muslims as a more or less insular community, whose needs do not intersect with those of the broader society. In this case, the needs of the city are held as primary and the needs of the local Muslims as secondary, if they are considered at all. In fact, several candidates justified their numerical rating with a short comment: "Helsinki does not need a grand mosque." However, to quote Sicinius in Shakespeare's *Coriolanus* (Act 3, Scene 1), "What is the city but the people?" Whether the Muslims of Helsinki were (implicitly or explicitly) included among the inhabitants of the city varied between the responses. Perhaps not surprisingly, recognition of Muslims as inhabitants was often associated with a positive attitude towards the mosque plan.

> Muslims have the same right to practise their religion as all other people living in Helsinki. (Female, Left Alliance, 5)

> Everyone who lives in Helsinki, no matter their religion, has the right to practise religion in suitable premises, so I support the building of a grand mosque. (Female, Feminist Party, 4)

> In my opinion, the grand mosque should be built because it has a big influence on the daily well-being of many people living in Helsinki. (Female, National Coalition Party, 4)

> It [the mosque] would not serve the interests of the people of Helsinki. (Male, Centre Party, 1)

However, even those candidates who explicitly included Muslims among the inhabitants of Helsinki very seldom perceived overlaps between the needs of the

---

[2]It is also worth noting that mosques in Europe have adopted functions that are very different from those of mosques in Muslim-majority countries but similar to those of European churches. European mosques, for example, increasingly perform ceremonies such as weddings and funerals. Allievi (2009, 21) refers to this as the "Christianization" of mosque functions.

Muslim community and those of the broader society. Indeed, only a few commentators considered the possibility that it could be in the interests of the city and state if the mosque was built. The few exceptions included the following:

> With the help of a grand mosque, especially the young people with asylum status could possibly be supported in their integration into Finland, and therefore it could be good for Helsinki if implemented right. (Male, Centre Party, 4)
>
> A grand mosque would enable dialogue between religions and, through that, increasing understanding. (Female, Left Alliance, 5)
>
> The mosque increases the value and diversity of the real estate. (Female, Left Alliance, 4)
>
> It is important that an urban environment that is built in central locations be open and shared by all. Hence, I hope that there will be, for example, suitable restaurants and other services in connection with the mosque. (Male, Green League, 4)

Thus, to summarize, the candidates declared overall support for freedom of religion but were hesitant to apply it to the project at hand. Some candidates even questioned whether the mosque project—or Islam, for that matter—is about religion at all. Instead of being a site of religious practice, the mosque was perceived as a political arena and channel through which foreign conflicts could seep into Finnish society. The possible benefits of the mosque to the city as a whole were ignored by all but a few respondents. In contrast, those favourable to the mosque plan tended to emphasize the equivalence of a church to a mosque as well as the needs of the local Muslim community.

4   Undefined Fears and Vague Worries

Sociologist of religion Allievi (2009, 60; 2014) has analysed European mosque debates and noted that the resistance to mosques can be roughly divided into two categories. On one hand, people are against mosque plans because of the concrete effects that mosques are supposed to have—for example, property value decline, noise, increased traffic, and violent crime. On the other hand, mosques are opposed for cultural reasons, for example, because of perceiving Islam as oppressive to women or otherwise incompatible with European values.

Our data contained examples of both kinds of worries. Quite frequently, however, the actual reasons for the opposition and suspicion were not stated, and the candidates only made vague references to general feelings of worry and concern. Usually the vagueness appeared to stem from a lack of information, especially about the funding sources, but it can also be asked whether at least some of these statements stem from common stereotypes concerning Islam. Be it as it may, if we follow Dinham and Jones (2010, 6), a religiously literate person acts based on knowledge, not on stereotypes.

> I feel suspicious about the construction of a grand mosque. (Male, Christian Democrats, 2)
>
> Concerns are raised about the mosque funding that possibly comes from outside Finland. (Female, Christian Democrats, 3)

The project funding from Bahrain raises questions. (Male, Social Democratic Party, 1)

Funding concerns [me] a lot, too. (Male, National Coalition Party, 2)

At other times, vague statements seemed to imply an underlying presupposition of shared knowledge. The candidates' choice of words expressed confidence in readers knowing beforehand about similar mosques in other countries and about the problems caused by them. The impression was that candidates did not explicate their concerns because they thought it was unnecessary, since readers would get the point.

For an electoral candidate, the avoidance of explicit accusations against Islam may provide protection against being labelled a bigot. Only hinting at problems, instead of naming them outright, allows for some leeway if one is called to answer for one's words.

Experiences from other countries are very bad. (Male, Finns Party, 1)

Experiences from elsewhere are not encouraging. (Male, National Coalition Party, 2)

Grand mosque plans have sadly turned out to be projects by the kind of actors whose aims are not good for the traditional way of life of us Finns. (Male, National Coalition Party, 1)

As illustrated by some of the examples, the electoral candidates often made references to bad experiences around mosques in other countries. Typically, however, the mosques and countries in question were not specified. References to experiences from other countries nevertheless illustrate the transnational aspects of mosque debates. In particular, the arguments used against the building of mosques are often borrowed from other national contexts. (See Allievi 2009, 52–53.) Cautionary tales of extremist mosques are circulated on discussion forums and shared on Facebook. Eventually the tales become disconnected from their original context and turn into common folklore among right-wing nationalists in Europe. Like fables and fairy tales, they are not set in a specific time or place, but serve as a general warning about all mosques.

5   Conclusion

When quoting the candidates, we have included their party and gender. All in all, however, such identities appeared to play a small role in the way that arguments for or against the mosque were constructed. Similar arguments were used across party lines, and where there were differences, they were of emphasis, not of kind. Christian Democrats, for example, were especially keen to emphasize the Christian heritage of Finland and the foreignness of Islam, but parallel views appeared in statements across the political spectrum. Altogether, it appears that the discourses presented above are common ways of discussing Islam and not limited to certain political stances. This further supports the argument that the statements analysed here reflect not just the views of individual Finnish politicians, but ideas that are relatively widespread in Finnish society—or in Europe more generally, as discussed in the previous paragraph.

A key issue dividing the statements is whether Islam is just one religion among many or whether it is a special case. Those favourable to the mosque tended to perceive it as a "Muslim church" and therefore subject to the same laws and regulations as any other house of worship. Those opposing the mosque, in turn, tended to treat Islam as unique.[3] Islam was perceived as a non-Finnish ideology that threatens to import foreign conflicts into the country. Because of its association with conservative social values and inegalitarianism, some commentators even denied Islam the status of a religion. Such a perception of Islam is, of course, very one-sided and blind to significant religious variation.

Even though the majority of the statements in the data do not explicitly promulgate this kind of alienating discourse, they fail to provide a counter-discourse to it. Perhaps the most typical stance taken in the data is that of "detached suspicion", where the affairs of the Muslim community are seen as being of little relevance to the policymakers. In this case, the only reasons for city officials to be interested in the whole mosque issue are their suspicions surrounding the funding sources and a desire to reserve the same lot of land for some other purpose (for example, apartments). Furthermore, very few statements mention the possibility of a mosque—or Muslims in general—making a valuable contribution to society. This obviously constitutes an additional blind spot in the mosque discussion.

From a religious literacy perspective, treating Islam as a special case is problematic, but so is treating it as a faith like any other. Religious literacy involves the ability to discern both the similarities and differences between—*and within*—religions. Therefore, simplified characterizations that either equate all religions or define them through opposition should be avoided. Religions are better understood as "pools of stories" (see Pauha and Jasinskaja-Lahti 2013) or as "baskets" (Hjärpe 1997), being collections of disparate and often conflicting narratives, norms, beliefs, and rituals. When crafting their religious identities, religious communities and individual believers choose some things from the basket and leave others. From this perspective, it is fruitless to debate whether Islam is fundamentally a religion of peace or a religion of war. The Islamic basket contains grounds for both interpretations. The mistake made in many of the statements analysed here is in seeing only some contents of the basket and confusing it with the basket as a whole.

What, then, could be done to correct some of the blind spots outlined in this paper? Drawing on Moore's (2015) approach to religious literacy, we would make four suggestions. (1) Like Moore, we want to emphasise the internal diversity of religion. This aspect is often missing in the data. Davie's repeated observation of "a lamentable quality of conversation about religion" in Britain (Dinham 2015, 45) applies, at least up to a certain point, to Finnish public discussions on Islam. Perceptions of Islam and Muslims are all too often based on media images that tend to exaggerate violence and terror. News from conflict zones provide a partial glimpse into Islam, but certainly not

---

[3]Other researchers have also noted (and critiqued) "the snare of exceptionalism" with regard to Islam and mosques in Europe (Cesari 2005, 2007; see also Allievi 2009, 7–9). Instead of treating Islam and Muslims as one religion or minority group among many, policymakers—and also some academics—are prone to perceive them as an exception that needs to be considered separately from other minority and religious issues.

the whole truth (see also Francis et al. 2015, 128–129, on Muslims as a risk or threat). Religious literacy involves a critical attitude towards one-sided media coverage and preparedness to learn the "other side". In fact, as Lövheim (2012) has pointed out, there is a need for religious media literacy.

(2) Another key point raised by Moore is the changing nature of religion. Islam, for example, has gone a long way from being "an Arab religion" to being a collective noun for a diverse set of traditions all around the world. Islam is no longer a foreign religion in Finland, and it should not be treated as such. It is important to be aware of the transnational links between Finnish Muslims and the Middle East, but the role of such links should not be overstated. The relations between Finnish Muslim communities in particular cannot be explained only in terms of Middle Eastern politics.

(3) For Moore, it is important to perceive religion as permeating all aspects of social life. Religion is not, and cannot be, confined to its own separate domain. All initiatives that propose a total exclusion of religion from the public sphere are therefore doomed from the start. Typically, such initiatives place increasing restrictions on certain highly visible forms of religious practice, and at the same time turn a blind eye to other ways in which religion influences public life. For instance, the singing of hymns in school celebrations is often framed as a Finnish national tradition instead of a religious one, and the singing of hymns is thus considered to be permissible in school, even though the practice of religion in general is not. This, in turn, supports the hegemonic position of the dominant Lutheran Church (Taira 2019). A more nuanced understanding of religion and its role in public life may contribute to a more equal society.

(4) In a related vein, Muslims should not be perceived as an enclave isolated from the surrounding city. Muslims are very much part of the city, and what affects the Muslims affects the city. Furthermore, aside from being a Muslim house of worship, a grand mosque is also an important urban landmark. As such, it has functions that go beyond the religious. By organising training and social support, a grand mosque can fill the gaps left by other service providers. It may also attract tourists, host school visits, and serve as an information point for anyone interested in Islam. All these functions should be considered alongside the potential security risks posed by a grand mosque.

References

Allievi, S. (2009). *Conflicts over mosques in Europe: Policy issues and trends*. London: Alliance Publishing Trust.

Allievi, S. (2014). Mosques in Western Europe. In *Oxford Islamic studies online*. Retrieved March 16, 2019, from http://www.stefanoallievi.it/2014/07/mosques-in-western-europe/.

Brems, E. (Ed.). (2014). *The experiences of face veil wearers in Europe and the law*. Cambridge: Cambridge University Press.

Cesari, J. (2005). Mosque conflict in European cities: Introduction. *Journal of Ethnic and Migration Studies, 31*(6), 1015–1024.

Cesari, J. (2007). Muslim identities in Europe: The snare of exceptionalism. In A. Al-Azmeh, & E. Fokas (Eds.), *Islam in Europe. Diversity, identity and influence* (pp. 49–67). Cambridge: Cambridge University Press.

Davie, G., & Dinham, A. (2019). Religious literacy in modern Europe. In A. Melloni, & F. Cadeddu (Eds.), *Religious literacy, law and history. Perspectives on European pluralist societies* (pp. 17–28). London: Routledge.

Dinham, A. (2015). Grace Davie and religious literacy: Undoing a lamentable quality of conversation. In A. Day & M. Lövheim (Eds.), *Modernities, memory and mutations: Grace Davie and the study of religion* (pp. 45–58). Farnham: Ashgate.

Dinham, A., & Jones, S. H. (2010). *Religious literacy leadership in higher education: An analysis of key issues and challenges for university leaders*. Report. Religious Literacy Leadership in Higher Education Programme, York. Retrieved March 20, 2019, from http://research.gold.ac.uk/id/eprint/3916.

Francis, M., van Eck, A., & van Twist, D. (2015). Religious literacy, radicalisation and extremism. In A. Dinham & M. Francis (Eds.), *Religious literacy in policy and practice* (pp. 113–134). Bristol: Policy Press.

Hashas, M., de Ruiter, J. J., & Vinding, N. V. (Eds.). (2018). *Imams in Western Europe. Developments, transformations and institutional challenges*. Amsterdam: Amsterdam University Press.

Helsingin seurakuntayhtymä. (2018). *Jäsentietojen vuositilasto 2017*. Retrieved March 13, 2019, from https://www.helsinginseurakunnat.fi/material/attachments/Ivt3wLwql/vuositilasto_2017.pdf.

Hjärpe, J. (1997). What will be chosen from the Islamic basket? *European Review, 5*(3), 267–274.

Inge, A. (2016). *The making of a Salafi Muslim woman. Paths to conversion.* New York, NY: Oxford University Press.

Konttori, J. (2015). *Monsieur, näkemyksemme eivät ole samalta planeetalta! Poliittisen ja yhteiskunnallisen eliitin tulkintoja islamista ja kansallisesta identiteetistä musliminaisten pukeutumisesta käydyissä keskusteluissa 2000-luvun Ranskassa.* Uskontotiede 15. Helsinki: Helsingin yliopisto, uskontotiede.

Kääriäinen, K. (2011). Religion and state in Finland. *Nordic Journal of Religion and Society, 24*(2), 155–171.

Lövheim, M. (2012). Religious socialization in a media age. *Nordic Journal of Religion and Society, 25*(2), 151–168.

Martikainen, T., & Latvio, R. (2018). Efforts to establish an imam-training programme in Finland. In M. Hashas, J. J. de Ruiter, & N. V. Vinding, (Eds.), *Imams in Western Europe. Developments, transformations and institutional challenges* (pp. 411–430). Amsterdam: Amsterdam University Press.

Moore, D. L. (2007). *Overcoming religious illiteracy: A cultural studies approach to the study of religion in secondary education.* New York: Palgrave Macmillan.

Moore, D. L. (2015). Diminishing religious literacy: Methodological assumptions and analytical frameworks for promoting the public understanding of religion. In A. Dinham & M. Francis (Eds.), *Religious literacy in policy and practice* (pp. 27–38). Bristol: Policy Press.

Nilsson, P.-E. (2018). *Unveiling the French republic. National identity, secularism, and Islam in contemporary France.* Studies in critical research on religion (Vol. 7) Leiden: Brill.

Pauha, T. (2017). Praying for one umma: Rhetorical construction of a global Islamic community in the facebook prayers of young finnish Muslims. *Temenos: Nordic Journal of Comparative Religion, 53*(1), 55–84.

Pauha, T. (2018). *Religious and national identities among young Muslims in Finland: A view from the social constructionist social psychology of religion.* Helsinki: University of Helsinki.

Pauha, T., & Jasinskaja-Lahti, I. (2013). Don't ever convert to a Finn: Young Muslims writing about finnishness. *Diaconia: The Journal for the Study of Christian Social Practice, 4*(2), 172–193.

Pauha, T., & Konttori, J. (2019). Finland. In O. Scharbrodt, S. Akgönül, A. Alibašić, J. S. Nielsen, & E. Račius (Eds.), *Yearbook of Muslims in Europe 10* (pp. 230–245). Leiden: Brill.

Pauha, T., & Martikainen, T. (2017). *Lausunto Oasis-hankkeesta*. Turku: Siirtolaisuusinstituutti.
Raittila, P., & Maasilta, M. (2008). Silmäyksiä islamin esittämiseen suomalaisessa journalismissa. In T. Martikainen, T. Sakaranaho, & M. Juntunen (Eds.), *Islam Suomessa: Muslimit arjessa, mediassa ja yhteiskunnassa* (pp. 225–243). Helsinki: SKS.
Rohe, M. (2019). Germany. In O. Scharbrodt, S. Akgönül, A. Alibašić, J. S. Nielsen, & E. Račius (Eds.), *Yearbook of Muslims in Europe 10* (pp. 293–310). Leiden: Brill.
Sorsa, L. (2015). *Kirkkona valtiossa. Katsaus Suomen evankelis-luterilaisen kirkon valtiosuhteen edellytyksiin ja uudistuspaineisiin*. Tampere: Kirkon tutkimuskeskus.
Taira, T. (2010). Religion as a discursive technique: The politics of classifying Wicca. *Journal of Contemporary Religion, 25*(3), 379–394.
Taira, T. (2013). The category of 'invented religion': A new opportunity for studying discourses on 'religion'. *Culture and Religion, 14*(4), 477–493.
Taira, T. (2019). Suvivirsi ja kristinuskon "kulttuuristuminen" katsomuksellisen monimuotoisuuden aikana. *Uskonnontutkija-Religionsforskaren, 8*(1). https://doi.org/10.24291/uskonnontutkija. v8i1.83000.
van der Veer, P. (1996). Writing Violence. In D. Ludden (Ed.), *Contesting the nation: Religion, community, and the politics of democracy in India* (pp. 250–269). Philadelphia: University of Pennsylvania Press.

Laestadians in the Public Sphere: Reading the Biggest Christian Revival Movement in Finland

Tapio Nykänen and Aini Linjakumpu

Abstract In this chapter, we argue that the political and economic activities of the members of the Conservative Laestadianism are often intertwined with the religion and the religious notions of the movement. Many seemingly secular stances and procedures have theological basis, while others rely and utilize the social networks that originate in the church. However, the effects of the religion in the secular life of Laestadians are quite diverse, and one should not oversimplify them. The implications of a person's religious background can be positive for the members of the movements and society as a whole, but the religious dimension can also have negative consequences in politics and business, especially in the context of strong social relationships, bonds, and reciprocal links. Religious literacy means, at least partly, that one recognizes the variable roles that religion has in different social contexts.

Keywords Laestadianism · Revival movement · Politics · Economics · Networks

1 Introduction

Conservative Laestadianism is the biggest revival movement within the Finnish Lutheran Church and the largest Christian revival movement in Scandinavia. Currently, the movement has approximately 100,000–120,000 followers in Finland and Sweden and some 5,000 in the United States and Canada. The movement is the biggest branch of *Laestadianism*, a pietistic revival movement that was born on the spiritual legacy of the Swedish-Sámi priest, preacher and botanist Lars Levi Laestadius (1800–1861).

Most branches of Laestadianism are theologically relatively similar to each other but socially more or less separate, independent and exclusive. This is also the case with Conservative Laestadianism (CL). The movement's established theology represents Conservative Laestadianism as *the* Christianity, and holds that the true Kingdom of God exists solely within the CL community. Hence, salvation can only be found through actual, active engagement with this true church. Other branches of

T. Nykänen (✉) · A. Linjakumpu
University of Lapland, Rovaniemi, Finland
e-mail: tapio.nykanen@ulapland.fi

© The Author(s) 2020
T. Sakaranaho et al. (eds.), *The Challenges of Religious Literacy*,
SpringerBriefs in Religious Studies, https://doi.org/10.1007/978-3-030-47576-5_3

Laestadianism are considered aberrant and are rejected as offering false hopes. In the Conservative Laestadian view, the Lutheran Church, in turn, offers "protection" from "the world" but not more: true faith and salvation are only found in the parish of Conservative Laestadians (the *ecclesiola in ecclesia* principle).

In this chapter, we will introduce two new perspectives on Conservative Laestadianism. First, we scrutinize the *political culture* associated with Laestadianism in its core support areas in the City of Oulu and its environs. By political culture we refer to the habits and procedures typical of the political behavior of Conservative Laestadians in the region. We begin by introducing the historical-theological basis for Laestadian politics and then go on to describe two empirical examples in a more detailed way: voting in elections and participating in municipal politics as elected council members.

Second, we examine the *business networks* of Conservative Laestadians. We focus especially on the way that religion functions as a resource for business. The analysis shows that the economic activity of Conservative Laestadianism is linked to and benefits in many ways from the doctrines of the movement as well as the social practices and the existing relationships. Among Conservative Laestadians, a theological understanding supports participation in economic activities, and the movement's social networks feature simultaneously as part of the economic activity.

In terms of religious literacy, this chapter aims at understanding how Conservative Laestadianism positions itself and how its members are acting in seemingly non-religious spheres, i.e. how to understand religiousness in political and economic contexts. We argue that the political and economic dimensions of the Laestadian world are not separate or self-sufficient. Instead, they are—sometimes quite visibly—intertwined with the religion and the religious notions of the movement (see Moore 2015, 31). There are, for example, procedures and guiding principles that have explicit religious connotations. Moreover, religious networks are sometimes clearly embedded in "secular" networks, especially in business life (see Granovetter 1992).

This approach challenges the positions interpreting religious groups or members of religious groups solely from the perspectives of religion or spirituality. When researching religious groups, it is important to realize that the interaction between religious and non-religious spheres can be complex and could even challenge the very idea of religiousness. This understanding is crucial since there are several disputes regarding the manner in which Conservative Laestadians and other conservative religious groups act in society. In this way, "'being literate' suggests that one is knowledgeable about religions and able to navigate the complexities of religious domains" (Biesta et al. 2019, 3).

We have gathered research material for the project during the period 2015–2018. The primary material consists of 39 interviews with politicians, entrepreneurs, office holders and other stakeholders, who had experience in local politics, business or both. The emphasis of the material is on the interviews of Laestadian informants. In addition to formally organized interviews, we have had informal discussions or consultations with some 40-50 Laestadian and non-Laestadian informants around the region.

Moreover, we have gathered material produced by the media, register data, material produced by the Conservative Laestadian movement, as well as material drawn from historical and genealogical sources.[1]

2 Laestadian Politics—Historical and Theological Basis

The official religious doctrine of Conservative Laestadianism has valued politics and political participation at least since the early 20th century (Talonen 1988; Nykänen 2012, 2016). Theologically, the positive approach has originated in the Lutheran two kingdoms doctrine. According to the doctrine, religious (divine) and secular power are separated, but also secular power gains its legitimacy from God. Because of this, a true believer should support secular authorities in everyday life—even if the authorities are sometimes misguided and make decisions that are problematic from the religious perspective (Nykänen 2012, 2016, 133–175). However, this does not mean that one should refrain from criticizing authorities entirely: Criticism is allowed but it should be moderate and reasonable, which means that a Laestadian should not act in a disruptive way (Nykänen 2016).

In fact, the movement has encouraged a constructive attitude towards society. It means that a believer should be an active citizen who does his/her best to enhance the prosperity[2] of the hometown. In practice, one should, for example, participate actively in working life and vote regularly in elections. Participation in business life is also associated with this approach.

In the 19th century, the movement often gave very precise instructions on how Laestadians should vote and, in particular, how they should *not* vote. The political left as a whole was considered problematic because of its atheistic and revolutionary background. Also, supporting the Finnish Rural Party was condemned in the 1960s because its politics was deemed disruptive (Nykänen 2012, 2016). Perhaps the most imperative and explicit restrictions were issued in the 1960s and 1970s. Back then, the movement struggled with internal divisions that were catalyzed by arguments between the movement's priests and leading laymen and by the general modernization and liberalization of Finnish society (Linjakumpu 2012). The movement's leadership tried to contain the situation by tightening internal discipline, which led to a more explicit control over political behavior as well.

In the early 1980s, the movement replaced its general instructions with a request to vote in elections. At the same time, politics and religion became more or less officially separated (Nykänen 2016). This was at least partially a counter-reaction to

---

[1]The themes of the chapter are examined more deeply on Nykänen and Harjumaa (2019) and Linjakumpu (2018).

[2]This interpretation originates in the book of Jeremiah: "Every human being, a religious one among others, lives and works in the context of one's own time and culture. But even the ones who were forced to move and lived their life in Babylonia 2,500 years ago, received a request from God, passed on by the prophet Jeremiah: 'Also, seek the peace and prosperity of the city to which I have carried you into exile' (Jer. 29:7)" (Hintikka 2008, 134–135).

the distressing atmosphere of the two previous decades. However, the old political stance prevailed, and it still does in the late 2010s. Exact support numbers are not available,[3] but all studies strongly suggest that the members still tend to vote the moderate political right (Talonen 2019; Nykänen 2016). Our research suggests that The Centre Party is, as it has traditionally been, the most popular political choice amongst Laestadians in Finland. The second most popular choice seems to be the National Coalition Party (see also Talonen 2019).

3   Voting in the 21st Century

As was mentioned above, prior to the 1980s, it was a rather common practice within the movement to give explicit orders about which party to vote and, in particular, which party to avoid. Moreover, in some cases, believers were instructed to vote for a particular Laestadian candidate. This was an organized way to funnel votes to certain individuals (Nykänen 2012, 162). Based on our material, neither of these is happening in the 2000s—at least not in such an overt manner. This, however, does not mean that the members of the movement would not talk about politics and political candidates. They do so, but usually the discussions are not arranged by any of the movement's organizations, such as the central organization SRK or the local congregations. Instead, political discussions are more or less spontaneous and carried out from bottom up. The most common exceptions are Laestadian politicians, who often campaign for themselves in Laestadian villages and municipalities. However, official rallies are not organized in parish houses or during religious events. As one interviewee stated, "the Centre Party is not the same thing as the Kingdom of God".

All of our interviewees, regardless of their relation to the movement, claimed that Laestadians still usually prefer other Laestadians in voting. It is not imperative to vote for a Laestadian, but based on our material, it is a common practice. The most typical explanation for this was that another believer shares similar values and can, therefore, be expected to generally act in a desirable way in politics. As a Laestadian politician put it, another Laestadian "might think similarly, a conviction somehow represents thoughts in general".

Another interviewee, a politician who had recently left the movement, pointed out that sometimes Laestadian values do also have a concrete effect on politics. The doctrine of the movement takes a negative view on particular social and cultural practices, such as open expressions of sexuality, consuming alcohol and competing in sports.[4] When a Laestadian votes for another Laestadian, he/she can expect that the candidate would not spend too much tax money for example on "building an

---

[3]Tapio Nykänen attempted to conduct a survey of the political opinions of Laestadians in 2011 during their annual summer gathering called *Suviseurat*. The movement's central organization SRK did not give permission to conduct the survey. According to the movement, *Suviseurat* is a religious meeting, and politics should not be mixed with religion.

[4]Physical activity is not problematic as such—especially young Laestadians are often quite active in playing games such as volleyball or basketball and generally exercising together. Competitive

open-air dance pavilion or financing a sports club". The interviewee also claimed that many older members of the movement often vote for another believer simply because the community has traditionally recommended so.

Many of our interviewees pointed out that there are only so many Conservative Laestadians and that the religious community is quite close-knit. Word about qualified and popular candidates spreads quickly in the network. It seems that nowadays votes concentrate on top candidates often through this semi-autonomous mechanism. In any case, the religious network can be seen as a valuable resource for Laestadian politicians, who can expect to get a significant number of votes from fellow believers. Nevertheless, according to several interviewees, it is quite rare that a Laestadian candidate would rely solely on fellow Laestadians' votes. There are usually multiple popular Laestadian candidates competing for the votes, and not all Laestadians can be expected to vote for Laestadian candidates. Especially in national elections Laestadian politicians usually campaign to appeal to a wider audience.

From the perspective of religious literacy, it is crucial to note that religious conviction and religious codes have effects on the Laestadian voting behavior and on the way Laestadian politicians campaign. However, religious context or religious rules of the community do not explain everything. Moreover, their role in voting and campaigning changes due time.

4   Being a Laestadian in Politics: Values and Cooperation

Finnish municipal politics often focuses on making practical decisions concerning the everyday lives of residents. Obviously, such decisions have a normative background, and, occasionally, the norms and values related to such decisions are debated openly. However, in connection with religious arguments, values are relatively rarely addressed in an open manner.

This does not, however, mean that religious values would be completely absent from municipal-level politics. As was stated earlier, religious notions may affect practical decisions such as "financing a dance hall or a sports club". In case of Conservative Laestadianism, religious values manifest themselves perhaps even more clearly through the general *style* of political action: Laestadians should act in a constructive way also in municipal politics (Nykänen 2012, 133–149). According to the interviewees, it means that "discussion and listening" are preferred to separation, let alone open conflict.

In addition to being constructive, actions taken by Laestadians are expected to contribute towards "the prosperity of the city". Hence, the general aim of political actions should be to benefit the local community, not to raise one's personal status or to increase the power of the party. What constitutes the good of the local community was often described in quite functional terms in the interviews. The interviewees

---

sports, in turn, are seen to require lots of attention and time, which may make it too difficult to practice the faith in proper ways.

reported that it is important to maintain a well-functioning school network, among other things. This can be considered family-oriented politics, and the family is, indeed, a crucial socioreligious institution in Laestadianism (Nykänen 2012, 133–148, 2016). The movement is strictly against birth control, and Laestadian families are still typically very large: it is not uncommon to have a family with more than ten children. Hence, society's support for large families in their everyday needs is very important to Laestadians. According to the interviewees, family-oriented thinking is often, if not always, clearly visible in the politics of Laestadian council members.

Even if Laestadian politicians do have some similarities in their political style and agenda, generally they were not seen to form independent or separate groups in councils. Instead, according to most interviewees, Laestadians and non-Laestadians alike, they primarily act as members of their political group in the council and can engage in cross-party cooperation as well. This was notable, as non-Laestadian interviewees and many other non-Laestadian informants described Laestadian communities generally as somewhat introvert and even cliquish. Some interviewees explained that a shared religion does not mean that the members of the movement would also have to share their political opinions. Furthermore, some of the interviewees said that religion is deliberately excluded from secular politics in order to ward off suspicions of the existence of inner circles. One Laestadian politician noted that Laestadians are usually a minority not only in the council but also in the political group, so cooperation with others is also a necessity.

If Laestadians do not generally form separate political groups in councils, are they still, to some degree, loyal to the religious community when acting in politics? Most interviewees claimed that, in politics, Laestadians are primarily loyal to the political party. However, there were also some contradictory statements. An interviewee who had left the movement stated that, in local politics, one should be clearly loyal to other Laestadians or at least other Laestadian politicians instead of the political party. Another politician, a younger Laestadian woman, stated that even though Laestadians are generally loyal to their party and not to the fellow believers in politics, things may get more complicated in some cases. According to the interviewee, especially older Laestadian men tend to think that they are "somewhat smarter" than younger female politicians. In some cases, this has meant that the interviewee in question has been expected to conform to the views of the older Laestadian politicians and to act as is "appropriate" in her role as a mother of a big family.

The above example shows how different networks may sometimes converge surreptitiously. Although politicians see themselves primarily as representatives of their party, the shared religious background of the older men and the younger woman in question seems to affect their relationship in a political context. The Conservative Laestadian community is quite patriarchal, especially in spiritual terms (for example, women are not accepted as priests or preachers), and the social norms that are constructed in religious contexts may well manifest themselves in secular interaction as well. This does not necessarily happen because the movement officially would require so: there are no religious rules that would make older men more competent than younger women in political decision-making. Instead, the example shows how social structures that originate in religion may sometimes have unofficial but still normative effects in secular life.

5 Economic Life: Religion as a Resource

In addition to being active in the political sphere, members of religious movements can be active economic actors (see e.g. Dana 2010). However, economics is generally not a core issue of religious movements or human spirituality: i.e. economic matters are not traditionally associated with the spiritual dimensions of human life. On the other hand, the combination of spirituality and economic concerns is often seen as a personal matter, and as such, affords some degree of discretion. On the surface, it does not seem appropriate to look at economic activity by associating it with religious belief, and the economic perspectives of religious movements or their members may seem rather marginal in comparison to their spiritual aspects.

Even though it may seem unusual at the outset to profile a religious movement through its engagement in economic activity, there are numerous religious movements in the United States, Europe and elsewhere with significant economic activity, and Finnish Conservative Laestadianism is quite similar to these in many respects (see Linjakumpu 2018, 15–18, 36–77; Dana 2010; Gauthier and Martikainen 2013; Kraybill and Nolt 2004). In the discussion that follows, Conservative Laestadianism is understood as a resource that influences and enables engagement in economic activity. The resourcefulness of Conservative Laestadians manifests itself in three ways: it is related to the (1) theology, (2) practices, and (3) social relationships of the movement. It is not economic activity as such that is of interest here but, rather, the *prerequisites* for it. We examine how Conservative Laestadianism as a network-like social entity endorses economic activity among the members of the movement.[5]

From the point of view of the religious literacy, the examination is essential because the complexity of religiousness and of the religious communality are identified in relation with the non-religious spheres of life. On the one hand, the religiousness does not determine the forms, conditions and prerequisites of the economic life straightforwardly but, on the other hand, religious communality plays an important role in the concretization of economic activity. Religious literacy implies the contextual articulation and interpretation of this role.

---

[5]By economic activity, we refer in particular to entrepreneurship and entrepreneurs. We also include economic activities such as working on company/institutional boards, issues of ownership, and holding responsible positions in companies.

6   Laestadian Theology as a Resource for Economics

Conservative Laestadianism, in particular *the central organization of Conservative Laestadians in Finland* (SRK), determines the theological interpretations adopted within the movement. These interpretations also apply to activities related to economics. Although entrepreneurship as a theological issue is not very common in Laestadian theological tradition, the subject is, however, addressed directly or in conjunction with employment, or earning or possessing money (Linjakumpu 2018, 109–116). As was stated earlier, Conservative Laestadianism is often associated with the Pietistic tradition, which was born within Lutheranism in the 17th century. In Pietism—as with other movements representing Protestant Ethics—the notion of work was strongly linked to the spiritual premises. According to Max Weber, Pietism in a way sought to secure salvation in secular professional life (Weber 1930/2005).

This Pietistic character is relatively easy to see in Laestadian theology. Work is a very common area of theological reflections in SRK's publications. Work is widely respected within the movement, and the theological considerations associated with it are abundant in the publications produced within the movement. Economic activity is an act of service that serves God, the family, and society. Entrepreneurship is a way of working whereby one earns a living for oneself and the family. It is also equated with taking responsibility—not just for oneself and the family but, by extension, for the well-being of society.

An entrepreneur can experience God's blessing through his/her engagement in economic life (see e.g. Lindgren 2011, 91). It can manifest itself as success, which is an indication of God's blessing for the entrepreneur and his/her actions. There may not be any outward justification for success, but the blessing comes as if it were a gift. The "dangers of mammon"—referring to greed, which makes money and ownership problematic—constitute the reverse side of the entrepreneurial blessing. In the theological sense, mammon—i.e. money and wealth—is an ambivalent topic, because in the Christian tradition, poverty often appears to be an acceptable, or even preferable, "condition" of a Christian person. The poors are blessed because they do not "have the stumbling block of mammon." (Hay 1989, 51.) However, the poor, or poverty, do not have a special role in the theology of Conservative Laestadians, i.e. poverty is not specifically referred to when discussing work or entrepreneurship.

Despite the risk of excessive mammon, pursuit of poverty is not specifically encouraged in Conservative Laestadian theology. Theology is rather giving an approval for entrepreneurship and earning money. In this sense, Conservative Laestadianism has similarities to the prosperity gospel (Linjakumpu 2018, 114). However, earning money is not a declared goal, but more like a matter that is not forbidden, but rather treated with "a cautious sympathy".

Theology of Conservative Laestadians is supporting—and resourcing—entrepreneurship and entrepreneurs. It embraces the idea that entrepreneurship as such is not problematic spiritually or in terms of conviction. Neither does it limit everyday business practices unless an entrepreneur is resorting to excess. In particular, the attitude towards money and ownership affects how entrepreneurship appears within the movement. If earning is seen as a theologically possible endeavor, it creates favorable conditions for entrepreneurship. By contrast, a positive attitude to entrepreneurship can produce a positive theological assessment of money and ownership, as is currently the case within the movement.

7 Religiously Motivated Practices as a Resource

In terms of religious literacy, it is crucial to understand that the theological tenets of a certain religious movement do not *directly* or *necessarily* affect the worldly life of a member of the movement. Instead, often theology constitutes a *potential* that directs and supports the members of religious movements. The potential can be concretized in the choices of life and in practical situations, but, at the same time, it is also possible that it is not realized in any way.

In addition to theology, what also matters is how the movement functions in practice. Conservative Laestadianism is indeed quite strongly based on practice, i.e. it is formed in and through existing practices whereby members of the movement are guided in desirable and acceptable directions. These practices are obviously often connected to the "official" theological basis of the movement, but sometimes the connection is quite loose and practices are rather based on social and organizational solutions. For this reason, it is interesting to investigate what forms of organizational support and approval for entrepreneurship emerge from Laestadianism.

One form of community-based support is linked to the official activity of the movement, that is to say, the ways in which official organizations close to SRK or SRK itself are promoting or advancing entrepreneurship. An important form of organizational support for entrepreneurship is the movement's weekly newspaper *Päivämies* in which articles, interviews and stories related to entrepreneurship and entrepreneurs appear frequently. In 2011, SRK also published a book on entrepreneurship. Entitled *Mitä jää viivan alle. Ajatuksia yrittäjyydestä* ("What's below the Line. Thoughts on Entrepreneurship"), the book includes 24 texts related to different aspects of entrepreneurship. The authors are entrepreneurs, some of whom are also known in public for their religious conviction and their membership of the movement. (See Tahkola and Niskanen 2011.)

In addition, the movement organizes entrepreneurial education at the Christian folk high schools it owns. Operating in three locations in Finland, the schools have slightly different study programs, but each school offers at least some entrepreneurship education. This entrepreneurship training, mainly targeted at Laestadian youth, has gained a fairly important role in the selection of education in these schools.

The folk high schools also offer so-called short courses. Some of these courses deal with entrepreneurship and are available in each of the three folk high schools. The entrepreneurial courses—unlike the entrepreneurial study programs—were originally intended mainly for business people and their spouses. The entrepreneurial courses are a well-established form of activity and they have been organized for decades. The number of participants has been rising steadily and, today, a total of over 100 persons in all schools participate in the courses annually. In addition to the general entrepreneurship courses, specialized courses have been arranged for female entrepreneurs, senior entrepreneurs and even for children. Furthermore, courses have been arranged for specific target groups such as bankrupt entrepreneurs, entrepreneurs in the ICT industry and rural entrepreneurs. (See Linjakumpu 2018, 118–122.)

Publishing and the activities of folk high schools are tangible ways in which the official organization of Conservative Laestadians supports entrepreneurship. In terms of business-related activities or publications, it is not a matter of the formal organization of the movement urging people of any age to become entrepreneurs. It is rather that entrepreneurship altogether seems to be embodied in the movement's activities and practices: for Conservative Laestadians, entrepreneurship appears as a "normal" and everyday matter, which is quite unconventional in the context of religious movements.

Through the activities related to entrepreneurship, Conservative Laestadians are able to build mutual trust, and in this way, the activities reinforce existing relationships between people and create new ones. They therefore support networking among people belonging to the movement, although it is not necessarily a declared goal. These relationships, efforts at building trust and working together can be seen as a resource for entrepreneurially oriented people (cf. Portes 1995; Rothstein 2005; Granovetter 1992). The organization builds a culture of entrepreneurship i.e. is creating preconditions for entrepreneurship.

When thinking of Conservative Laestadianism from the point of view of religious literacy, it is particularly important to be aware of the holistic and communal nature of the movement (see e.g. Hurtig 2013, 46). Practical support for entrepreneurs and entrepreneurship is part of the religious nature of Laestadianism. This is not a typical way of acting among religious groups. In case of less holistic or communal groups, there is no need for practices that are dealing with seemingly non-religious issues such as business life.

8   Social Dimensions and Networking as a Resource

Although entrepreneurship may often appear as a practice of pursuing individual goals and ideas, it is, however, essential to work with other people, i.e. customers, business partners, subcontractors, financiers and employees. The social dimension and the various relationships involved are essentially present in the implementation of business activities. Entrepreneurial activity is linked to various existing social networks and is therefore, by definition, a network-like practice. This starting point is also essential when examining business activities among Conservative Laestadians.

The network perspective provides conceptual tools for perceiving the importance of social contacts, communality and interdependence in the economic activity of people belonging to the movement. In this way, economic activity appears to be socially located and constructed. There is a wide range of contacts, interests and relationships between Conservative Laestadians in the context of economy. Following the ideas of Mark Granovetter, economic relationships have become embedded in social (and sometimes, political) networks (Granovetter 1992, 62–65). In other words, economics depends on the relationships and networks in which different forms of economics are located (see Johanson 2015, 206–207). It is based on social relationships, and it is linked to these relationships. It should be noted that these relationships are, in part, inevitably shaped by non-Laestadians, and in some cases, they can also largely determine the logic of economic activity.

The concept of embeddedness means that the social relationships and networks within the movement are part of the networks of economic activity or, more accurately, the economic networks of Conservative Laestadians overlap with—or are embedded in—other Laestadian networks. In practice, this means that Conservative Laestadianism as a whole is seen through social relations, as a relatively broad, and at the same time, a complex network entity of which economic networks are part.

The Conservative Laestadian way of life, the theological premises, and the practices of the spiritual community form a wide range of relationships that build networks. The local, regional and national practices of the movement contribute to building relationships. The local Associations of Peace, voluntary work, and bazaars intrinsically bring members of the organization together. Likewise, the regional or national activities run by the SRK offer similar opportunities beyond the local level. Summer services, regional services, speaker meetings, congregational days, large-scale courses and publishing activities create contacts and relationships among a substantial number of people. (Cf. Nykänen 2012, 96–109, 198–215; Hurtig 2013, 46–47.)

In addition to the "official" activities, unofficial practices build relationships between people. The members of the movement spend time with each other: hobbies, neighborly help, and other informal communication between families, friends and acquaintances are creating and maintaining social relationships. In all of these situations, people meet other people, create relationships and trust, share information and maintain friendship and acquaintance.

Therefore, the socially active Conservative Laestadian lifestyle creates, as if naturally, networks between people. Networks built on concrete activities are encouraged directly or indirectly in the doctrine of the movement. This way of life is strengthened by the official doctrine of the movement, in which the joint activities between the Associations of Peace, the families, and the other members of the movement are seen in a positive light.

When Conservative Laestadianism is understood as a network of different relationships, economically relevant relations are part of—or overlap with—all other relationships, i.e. economic networks are therefore not a separate or autonomous part of the other networks and relationships of the movement. Economic actors do not work in a social vacuum: networks link economic actors with social interaction (Johanson 2015, 207). This means that, for example, an entrepreneur cannot merely think of, or pursue, his or her own interests and profit in the context of economic activity, but must also take into account the prerequisites imposed by the social environment. However, networks are not coercive or mandatory structures that define the content of an activity and the variety of choices that may be made. Rather, they tend to provide structures that can be employed in many different ways in economic concerns. (See e.g. Portes 1995, 12.)

In terms of religious literacy, in strongly communal religious movements, economic activity is not separate from relationships among the members of those movements, but they are essentially linked to each other. Thus, the effect of religion on business activities cannot be understood without the existence of social relations and networks. It should be noted, however, that the importance of these relations is not the same for all people: benefits brought by the relations vary from person to person.

9 Conclusion

In this chapter, we have analyzed the engagement of Conservative Laestadian people in the political and economic spheres, or in the movement's own terms, "the world". The research results help to understand the connection of religion to economics and politics. We have taken particular care not to "religiousize" the Laestadian people, i.e. not to see Laestadians only as Christian devotees. Instead, Laestadianism in "the world" is interpreted as a social movement inspired by its spiritual background, but simultaneously, as a movement functioning in the domains of earthly life.

An additional purpose of this chapter has been to draw attention to the fact that research on economics and politics is at least partly blind to religion. Economics and politics are sometimes seen as secular territories where religion has no significance. The chapter outlines the religiousness of these areas: how religion is structured in the areas of non-religious life, i.e. politics and economics.

To conclude, there are at least two mechanisms that mediate the effects of the "religious faith" in the worldly dimension as well. First, there are some fundamental theological/religious values that explicitly affect the secular life of Laestadians. These include, for example, the demand to not act disruptively but in a constructive way, benefitting one's "hometown". Also, some regulations concerning open sexuality and the use of alcohol are based explicitly on religious doctrines. Both value-sets are visible in Laestadian politics. In business, the theological norms perhaps serve more as a resource: they enable and support acting in business life.

Second, religious and religion-related networks are embedded in the secular—such as political and economic—ones. In other words, people who know each other from religious or religion-related networks easily form networks and enter into co-operation in other contexts as well, such as voting in elections or doing business together. These forms of co-operation may not be best described as "religious" in the common—or even theoretical—sense of the word, but they can be seen as having roots in religion and religious networks.

It should be noted here that the relationship and interaction of religion, or the religious community, and economy can also be examined from the opposite perspective. In other words, religion does not only have an effect on economic matters, but economic matters do also affect the religious community. This can be illustrated through an illuminating example offered by Adam Dinham. Before the modern welfare state, welfare used to be strongly the provenance of churches (Dinham 2015). Among other effects, this relation engaged people to the parishes very effectively. Once the relation was broken, churches lost some of their practical meaning in people's lives. In Conservative Laestadianism, the parish is still strongly connected to welfare, or to be exact, to the material wealth and well-being. In practice, religion-based networks help people in their everyday life: they offer several kinds of social capital, business opportunities and political support (see Furbey et al. 2006). The embeddedness of the networks is not necessarily the reason for being a devotee, as one can stay for example in the business networks after leaving the religious community. However, it creates cohesion and strengthens the religious network. When several good things originate in the community, one does not want to leave it.

Based on our work, religious literacy means, at least, sensitivity to understand the role of religion in non-religious contexts and in various social relationships and structures. This implies that a religiously literate person also recognizes the diversity of the effects of religion on social life. The implications of a person's religious background can be positive for the members of the movements and society as a whole, but the religious dimension can also have negative consequences in politics and business, especially in the context of strong social relationships, bonds, and reciprocal links. Hence, social, political and economic effects of religion are seldom (if ever) one-dimensional. Instead, they are variable and different in changing contexts.

References

Biesta, G., Aldridge, D., Hannam, P., & Whittle, S. (2019). *Religious Literacy: A way forward for religious education?* A Report Submitted to the Culham St Gabriel's Trust. Retrieved November 14, 2019, from https://www.reonline.org.uk/news/religious-literacy-a-way-forward-for-religious-education/.

Dana, L.-P. (Ed.). (2010). *Entrepreneurship and religion*. Cheltenham: Edward Elgar.

Dinham, A. (2015). Religious literacy and welfare. In A. Dinham & M. Francis (Eds.), *Religious literacy in policy and practice* (pp. 101–112). Bristol: Policy Press.

Furbey, R., Dinham, A., Farnell, R., Finneron, D., & Wilkinson, G. (2006). *Faith as social capital: Connecting or dividing?* Bristol: The Policy Press.

Gauthier, F., & Martikainen, T. (2013). Acknowledging a global shift. A primer for thinking religion in consumer societies. *Implicit Religion, 3,* 261–276.

Granovetter, M. (1992). Economic action and social structure: The problem of embeddedness. In R. Swedberg & M. Granovetter (Eds.), *The sociology of economic life* (pp. 53–81). Boulder: Westview Press.

Hay, D. A. (1989). *Economics today. A Christian critique.* Leicester: Apollos.

Hintikka, M. (2008). Työn aika. In K. Hyry & M. Leppänen (Eds.), *Työssä, levossa* (pp. 127–137). Oulu: Suomen Rauhanyhdistysten Keskusyhdistys ry.

Hurtig, J. (2013). *Taivaan taimet. Uskonnollinen yhteisöllisyys ja väkivalta.* Tampere: Vastapaino.

Johanson, J.-E. (2015). Heikot suhteet ja uppoutuneisuus. In K. Eriksson (Ed.), *Verkostot yhteiskuntatutkimuksessa* (pp. 196–213). Helsinki: Gaudeamus.

Kraybill, D. B., & Nolt, S. M. (2004). *Amish enterprise. From plows to profits.* Baltimore: The Johns Hopkins University Press.

Lindgren, K. (2011). Vastuullinen taloudenhoito. In M. Niskanen, & J. Tahkola (Eds.), *Ajatuksia yrittäjyydestä. Mitä jää viivan alle* (pp. 88–91). Oulu: Suomen Rauhanyhdistysten Keskusyhdistys ry.

Linjakumpu, A. (2012). *Haavoittunut yhteisö. Hoitokokoukset vanhoillislestadiolaisuudessa.* Tampere: Vastapaino.

Linjakumpu, A. (2018). *Vanhoillislestadiolaisuuden taloudelliset verkostot.* Tampere: Vastapaino.

Moore, D. L. (2015). Diminishing religious literacy: Methodological assumptions and analytical frameworks for promoting the public understanding of religion. In A. Dinham & M. Francis (Eds.), *Religious literacy in policy and practice* (pp. 27–38). Bristol: Policy Press.

Nykänen, T. (2012). *Kahden valtakunnan kansalaiset. Vanhoillislestadiolaisuuden poliittinen teologia.* Rovaniemi: Lapland University Press.

Nykänen, T. (2016). The Political Trinity of Conservative Laestadianism: God, His Kingdom and Authorities. *Political Theology.* https://doi.org/10.1179/1462317X15Z.000000000175.

Nykänen, T., & Harjumaa, T. (2019). Vanhoillislestadiolaisuus Pohjois-Suomen kunnallispolitiikassa. In A. Linjakumpu, T. Nykänen, T. Harjumaa, & S. Wallenius-Korkalo (Eds.), *Politiikka, talous ja työ. Lestadiolaisuus maailmassa* (pp. 59–91) Rovaniemi: Lapland University Press.

Portes, A. (1995). Economic sociology and the sociology of immigration: A conceptual overview. In A Portes, (Ed.), *The economic sociology of immigration. Essays on networks, ethnicity, and entrepreneurships* (pp. 1–41). New York: Russell Sage Foundation.

Rothstein, B. (2005). *Social traps and the problem of trust.* Cambridge: Cambridge University Press.

Tahkola, J., & Niskanen, M. (2011). Lukijalle. In M. Niskanen, & J. Tahkola, (Eds.), *Mitä jää viivan alle. Ajatuksia yrittäjyydestä* (p. 7). Oulu: Suomen Rauhanyhdistysten Keskusyhdistys ry.

Talonen, J. (1988). *Pohjois-Suomen lestadiolaisuuden poliittis-yhteiskunnallinen profiili 1905-1929.* Helsinki: Suomen kirkkohistoriallinen seura.

Talonen, J. (2019). Lestadiolaisuus, politiikka ja eduskuntavaalit 2015. In A. Linjakumpu, T. Nykänen, T. Harjumaa, & S. Wallenius-Korkalo (Eds.), *Lestadiolaisuus maailmassa. Politiikka, talous ja työ* (pp. 23–58). Rovaniemi: Lapland University Press.

Weber, M. (1930/2005). *The Protestant ethic and the Spirit of Capitalism.* Routledge: London.

Challenges of Religious Literacy in Education: Islam and the Governance of Religious Diversity in Multi-faith Schools

Inkeri Rissanen, Martin Ubani, and Tuula Sakaranaho

Abstract This chapter seeks take part in an emerging research where religion is approached as a whole school endeavor. Previous research and policy recommendations typically focused on teaching about religion in school, but the accommodation of religious diversity in the wider school culture merits more attention. Based on observations in our multiple case studies, we discuss the multi-level governance of religious diversity in Finnish multi-faith schools with a particular focus on the challenges of religious literacy for educators. The three examples we present focus on the inclusion of Muslims in Finnish schools and in particular on the challenges for educator (1) in interpreting the distinction between religion and culture, (2) in recognizing and handling intra-religious diversity, and (3) in being aware of Protestant conceptions of religion and culture. A theme cutting across these examples is how they reflect the tendencies either to see different situations merely through the lens of religion (religionisation), or not to recognize the importance of religion at all (religion-blindness). We argue that religious literacy should be recognized and developed as a vital part of the intercultural competencies of educators.

Keywords Multi-faith schools · Religious diversity · Governance · Religious literacy · Islam

1 Introduction

During recent decades, Finnish society has become increasingly multicultural and multireligious. Due to this there have been some changes to Finnish legislation, so that the Freedom of Religion Act was renewed, together with acts for basic, secondary and

I. Rissanen (✉)
Tampere University, Tampere, Finland
e-mail: inkeri.rissanen@tuni.fi

M. Ubani
University of Eastern Finland, Joensuu, Finland

T. Sakaranaho
University of Helsinki, Helsinki, Finland

© The Author(s) 2020   39
T. Sakaranaho et al. (eds.), *The Challenges of Religious Literacy*,
SpringerBriefs in Religious Studies, https://doi.org/10.1007/978-3-030-47576-5_4

upper-secondary schools, at the beginning of the twenty-first century (see Sakaranaho 2013). Thus, the growing diversity of Finnish society has been acknowledged by the state, and legal adjustments made accordingly, in education among other areas. On a more practical level, however, recent reports highlight that schools and teacher education in Finland have not adapted sufficiently to the changed demographics of Finnish society (Tainio and Kallioniemi 2019; Räsänen et al. 2018). An important part of this shift concerns the growing number of students belonging to different religions. In current research, religious diversity in education has mainly attracted attention in relation to religious education in state-supported schools (Sakaranaho 2013; Rissanen et al. 2019). Furthermore, while Europe-wide recommendations for policy and practices for teaching about religions in European schools have emerged (Jackson 2014; OSCE/ODIHR 2007), these do not address the accommodation of religious diversity in the wider school culture. Instead of maintaining the rather narrow focus on religious education, this chapter takes part in an emerging research where religion is approached as a whole-school endeavour (Ubani and Ojala 2018). Religion as a whole-school endeavour, moreover, will be discussed from the point of view of religious literacy and multi-level governance, which to date have not received enough attention in research on religious diversity and education in Finland. In doing so, it will widen the perspective of current international discussion on religious literacy that focuses on religious education to religious literacy in relation to a school community as a whole (cf. Biesta et al. 2019).

Religious literacy is about the ability to "discern and analyse the fundamental intersections of religion and social/political/cultural life through multiple lenses" (Moore 2015, 30). As a result of the process of secularisation in Europe, however, religious literacy as a civic competence is getting weaker or lacking altogether (Dinham and Francis 2015), resulting in a sort of illiteracy with regards to religion in public space. In the field of education, criticism of secular normativity (i.e. the othering of non-secular worldviews in educational thinking and practices) has emerged along with discussions about post-secular society (Berglund 2017; Poulter et al. 2016; Rissanen 2018). Finland can be described as a post-secular society in which the secular system of governance is encountering increasing religious diversity and a rising public presence of religion (see Nynäs et al. 2015). The Finnish state has official multicultural policies that extend to efforts to support different cultural and religious identities in schools. In practice, however, a gap exists between the official recognition of religious diversity by the state and the religious minorities' experiences of inclusion in schools (Rissanen et al. 2016; Rissanen 2018, 2019). It is our contention that discrepancies such as this invite an analysis of religious literacy as a relevant component in the skillset of education professionals in a post-secular context.

The challenge of religious literacy is apparent when looking at teachers and principals in Finland, for whom, as education professionals, religion seems to be a difficult matter to cope with. The struggle to come to terms with religion is particularly apparent in relation to growing religious diversity in Finnish schools, where Islam is seen as one of the main challenges. Contemporary education professionals have grown up and been educated in the rather monocultural atmosphere of Finland, which has not been the best environment for the development of religious literacy as a part of intercultural competence. It is also important to recognise that education professionals, on the main, share the position of the majority, possessing certain inherited cultural, ideological and religious values that shape their personal worldviews as well as the educational practices in general (Rissanen et al. 2015, 2016). However, due to growing cultural diversity in Finnish society, the state policies make demands on principals and teachers to come to terms with this diversity and fashion the management of teaching in schools accordingly. Moreover, principals and teachers in their everyday work are faced with pupils who, especially in the major cities in Finland, have grown up in a culturally diverse environment where different religiously based values, beliefs and practices (i.e. dress codes and dietary habits) are an elementary part of their everyday life at school. Consequently, in order for education professionals to successfully come to terms with and manage the growing religious diversity in Finnish schools, it is important to develop their intercultural skills—and religious literacy as a part of those skills.

Due to rapid social changes, intercultural competence has in recent decades become commonly acknowledged as a key component of education professionals' competence as an "ability to effectively and appropriately interact in an intercultural situation or context" (Berry and Southwell 2011, 453). In short, the focus of intercultural competence lies in encounters between persons with different identity markers in different contexts. However, with respect to Finland, the role of religion as an identity marker, and as a possible dimension of culture, has not received sufficient attention in research on multicultural education in general and on teachers' intercultural competence in particular (Rissanen et al. 2016). All in all, even though teachers in Finland are highly respected professionals with a strong ethical orientation and willingness to promote equality in education (Kuusisto et al. 2012), and the high quality of Finnish teacher education has become internationally recognised, developing teachers' abilities to deal with cultural and religious diversity can be underlined as an area that needs more attention.

Concerning intercultural competence, it is important to look at the challenges of religious literacy among education professionals (teachers and principals). We will investigate these in light of three examples from Finnish schools. These examples focus on the inclusion of Muslims in Finnish schools and, in particular, on the challenges in: (1) interpreting the distinction between religion and culture, (2) recognizing and handling intra-religious diversity, and (3) awareness of Protestant conceptions of religion and culture. A theme that cuts across these examples is how they reflect the tendencies either to see different situations merely through the lens of religion (religionisation) or not to recognise the importance of religion at all (religion-blindness).

Investigation of the aforementioned examples is based on qualitative data that we have collected in Finnish schools in our recent research projects. The first set of data concerns the inclusion of Muslims in Finnish and Swedish schools. Altogether 36 interviews were conducted with school principals (n = 10 in both countries) and Muslim parents (n = 8 in both countries), who were positioned as mediators or "cultural interpreters" in their school communities. This data was analysed from the perspective of negotiations regarding the inclusive citizenship of Muslims (Rissanen

2018) and different ideologies of diversity held by school principals (Rissanen 2019). The second set of data focuses on the discrepancies between educational policy and practice in issues related to the role of multiculturalism and religion in school. The data was collected in a school in the metropolitan area of Helsinki by means of ethnographic enquiry lasting one year, including interviews and observation. It also includes quantitative data based on different members of a school community. In addition, we also studied the policy documents concerning public education in Finland (Ubani 2013, 2018).

2   Public Schools and the Governance of Religious Diversity

Coming to terms with growing religious diversity in Finnish public schools involves different processes of governance, as the top-down policies implemented by the state are not enough. Instead, a pluricentric governance based on interdependence and negotiation is needed (see Torfing 2007; see Bell and Hindmoor 2009; Sakaranaho 2019). Hence, it is crucial to be aware of and look at different processes of steering and implementation of school policies, which are undertaken not only by the state but even more importantly by the municipalities and education professionals (see Sakaranaho and Martikainen 2015; Sakaranaho 2018, 2019).

Finland employs a Nordic type of state-supported comprehensive public education where the aim is the equal education of all members of society. The role of schools in implementing state policies on the governance of education has been discussed extensively in research that highlights the issues related to citizenship, social cohesion and the agenda of self-preservation of the nation-state (Mundy 2007; Weymann 2013). In the formation of the Nordic welfare state, a sense of nationhood has also been connected with the development of a strong public school system (Buchardt et al. 2013).

The basis for the current Finnish public education was developed in the 1860s during a period of Finnish national awakening. As part of this development, the responsibility for public compulsory education was shifted from the Evangelical Lutheran Church of Finland to the municipalities. From there on, comprehensive education in Finland has been an organic part of the state governance. The last extensive reform of the Finnish educational system was undertaken in the early 1970s, when the current system of comprehensive education was developed. In accordance with this, the whole population of Finland would study from 7 to 16 years of age in a uniform school system. (Sakaranaho 2013.)

The current Finnish curriculum for basic education articulates diversity as a feature of all students, and it demands the recognition of different religious and cultural identities. In comparison with the Swedish curriculum, which is rather silent about diversity and makes a distinction between the students' "own origins" and the "common heritage" (with the latter including "basic values of Swedish society") in a relatively essentialising manner, the discourse employed in the Finnish curriculum can be described as non-essentialist and multiculturalist (Zilliacus et al. 2017). Recent research has pointed out that the ideal of strengthening cultural diversity is one of the overarching aims of the current Finnish basic education system (Mäkelä et al. 2017). When compared with the previous National Core Curriculum for Basic Education (henceforth NCCBE), there is strong emphasis on culture in the current curriculum (NCCBE 2004, 2014; Ubani 2012). In the recent curriculum, students are to "be educated for a world that is diverse in terms of culture, language, religion and convictions" and to view "cultural diversity in principle as a positive resource" (NCCBE 2014, 21).

Similarly to the current national core curriculum, in general the Finnish state policy documents address issues regarding religious, cultural, linguistic and ethnic diversity (Ubani 2013; Sakaranaho 2013). In fact, as mentioned in the introduction, several reports have placed Finland among the leaders in Europe in integration policies and also in minority rights (Multiculturalism Policy Index 2010; Migrant Integration Policy Index 2015; Varjonen et al. 2017). However, there have been strong concerns about the implementation of such policies in practice (Fagioli-Ndlov 2015, 13). The higher-level policies act as a framework, while schools are one of the implementation contexts for how the national policies concerning multiculturalism and religion are interpreted by the municipalities.

The central role of the state notwithstanding, the daily management and operation of schools in Finland are municipality-based. Hence, the municipalities oversee the application of the generic national guidelines in the Basic Education Act issued by the Ministry of Education and Culture, from the descriptions of general goals and time allocation in instruction and the national core curriculum to daily practices in schools. In addition to state schools, the municipalities oversee private schools as well. (Vitikka et al. 2012; Ubani 2013.) The important role of the municipalities in relation to education is also evident in that municipalities in larger cities have their own guidelines concerning the management of religion in schools; therefore, guidelines may differ from one municipality to the next. As an example, one can cite the question of girls' swimming lessons or absences due to religious festivals. These guidelines may include booklets, in-service training for principals, teachers and other personnel, and maintaining an open or closed web portal. (Ubani 2018; Mäkelä et al. 2017.)

To sum up, when compared to many other European countries, Finnish educational policy is characterised by a rather uniform educational structure. In this system, the state officials at different levels of the administration interpret and implement the policies without much negotiation with civil society. However, the one special case in this quite uniform implementation system seems to be the governance of religious diversity in schools (see Sakaranaho 2018). In schools, principals act relatively autonomously when outlining the different practices. Therefore, there can be great variations in school practices with regards to religion in different public schools, even in the area of one municipality. Unlike in many other countries, in Finland there is no system of monitoring schools and their instruction. Instead, the educational system is based on trust in the professionalism of teachers (Husu and Toom 2012). This also gives room for principals to make individual decisions with regards to the handling of religions in their school that diverges from practices in neighbouring schools.

While in recent years there has been a policy-driven aim to increase civil participation in governance of different fields of society, in public education the autonomy
of the educational professionals remains rather uncontested. However, in order for
the governance of religious diversity to be in line with the general notion of trust
in the educational system, teachers' professionalism should incorporate religious
literacy as part of intercultural competence. The following examples analyse some
challenges in religious literacy among educational professionals and, accordingly,
highlight issues where it is in need of development.

3   Distinction Between Religion and Culture

In the current world, the relationship between religion and culture has become more
complex. On the one hand, new cultural paradigms emphasise the need to recognise
the fluidity and internal diversity of religions and individuality of their followers, but
the reaction to this has also been the "deculturalization of religion", with people of
faith defending the authenticity and universality of their tradition (Roy 2010). Thus,
distinguishing between religion and culture has political implications, and it demands
religious literacy. In the field of religious education, the way in which religions should
be represented and investigated in the classroom—as cultural phenomena or with a
focus on doctrines and truth claims—has been a much discussed issue. The cultural
approaches have been accused of misrepresenting religion in a way that does not
teach respect for differences (e.g. Wright 2004; Barnes 2006). By contrast, how the
ways of distinguishing between religion and culture steer the governance of religious
diversity in the larger school community is a less explored area, and it is our focus
here. We have observed how educators sometimes make distinctions between religion
and culture in a simplified and strategic manner. Some school principals legitimize
their assimilative demands by interpreting certain behaviour of parents or students as
"cultural" and, therefore, they reduce the importance of this behaviour and move it
outside the scope of religious freedom. In our studies, for instance, some principals
interpreted Muslim parents' unwillingness to shake hands with the opposite sex as
"only a cultural issue", and this interpretation was used as an argument to justify their
demand that adapting to the common way of greeting in the country is something
that can be expected from the parents (Rissanen 2019). Most of the Muslim parents
in our data did greet the opposite sex by shaking hands and did not consider this a
problem, but there were also those who regarded the choice to not touch the opposite
sex as a right based on their religious freedom.

As an example, one can mention a female principal who recollected how some
Muslim fathers were not willing to shake hands with her. When she was asked how
she handled the situation, she described that when a certain father had refused to
shake hands with her, at first she let him come to her office but later when the father's
unwillingness to shake hands with her continued, she did not invite him to her office
but instead had a discussion with him in the corridor as a sign of displeasure. It should
be noted that on no occasion did the principal in question explain to the father why

she behaved with him the way she did. It is evident that the principal associated not shaking hands with the unequal treatment of women and thus experienced it very negatively (Ubani forthcoming).

Religious literacy can facilitate awareness of different types of behaviour among Muslims but perhaps also more nuanced interpretations of the reasons, in this case, for not shaking hands. Instead of showing a lack of respect for the opposite sex, many of our Muslim informants interpreted not shaking hands with the opposite sex as an act of respect. Thus, the same behaviour can lead to opposite interpretations, and if there is no communication between the involved parties, it can cause grave misunderstandings and, in the worst cases, even conflict. The aim in developing religious literacy is to avoid such unfortunate outcomes.

On the other hand, we also observed occasions of where certain cultural issues were "religionised". Often the most identifiable and distinctive expression of what is considered religion—but is rather an interplay of religion, culture, ethnicity, nationality and minority position—becomes religionised and reified as a normative assumption. There were situations where teachers gave examples of frictions between Somali families in school, which in their view were based on religion—and Islam, in particular—but in reality were connected to clan division. The interpretations of these frictions also highlighted the way in which teachers see Somalis as a uniform group. A case in point happened when some Somali mothers came to the school and demanded that their daughters should not be allowed to play with some other Somali children. The teachers knew that the division in this conflict was based on clan membership but nonetheless interpreted that the incident was in fact caused by religion (specifically Islam). This particular case reflects a general tendency to explain conflicts and, more generally, any inappropriate behaviour of Muslim students solely in terms of religion and hence to 'religionise' their behaviour (Ubani 2015).

It has to be admitted that the problems of religionisation are recognised by some professionals in schools, who endeavour to overcome it by emphasising the irrelevance of Muslim identity. For example, many Finnish education professionals are critical toward the current separative approach to religious education for the reason that it makes Muslim identities "too visible" (Rissanen 2019). The ethos of secular normativity is exemplified by the fact that even many of those professionals who support the "celebration of diversity" in school leave religious identity markers out of it.

However, we noticed that there are clear differences in how distinctions between religion and culture are interpreted with respect to the (imagined) majority religion and minority religions. Protestant Christianity continues to play a significant (although continuously debated) role as an important source of tradition and as an identity marker in the school culture, whereas Islam hardly ever does. On the contrary, many principals perceived Islam as essentially religious and, therefore, not having pedagogical relevance as an aspect of cultural heritage or as an identity marker of the students that could be positively recognised. In other words, the intersections of religion with other identity markers is recognised in the case of the majority religion, but not in the case of Islam. The inability to recognise the role of Islam as a cultural element or identity marker also relates to principals' perceptions, according to which

"Islam is not a tradition here", reflecting a continued understanding of Islam as alien to the Nordic context. Due to this "secular Protestant normativity", in many Finnish schools Muslim identities thus become visible only through restrictions and the difficulties that their incorporation into the school culture entails. According to the views of Muslim parents and teachers, this makes it difficult to increase knowledge about Islam and counter the stigma attached to Muslim identities (Rissanen 2018, 2019).

4 Intra-religious Diversity

Another issue that is much discussed in the scholarly field of religious education but less explored as affecting an entire school is the recognition or misrecognition of intra-religious diversity. Representation of religions as monolithic entities can maintain stereotypes and prejudices, but it can also be used as a strategy to counter those by representing sympathetic and "sanitised" versions of religions (Revell 2012). We have observed the inability of educators to recognize intra-religious diversity in the everyday life of schools. As a result, religious diversity is governed in a way that does not offer justice to individual pupils and families and may even violate their freedom concerning religious convictions and expressions, as well as the heritage of their cultural and national origins. For instance, in a school with many Somali Muslims, "religion" easily equals "Islam" and "Muslim" equals "Somali". In this case, the Somali way of practising religion is regarded as an orthopraxis of Islam, the tenets of which all other Muslims are then expected to follow. In this type of school, Islam is sometimes regarded as an internal attribution that connotes aspects related to, for instance, challenges in social integration, language and learning. In concrete terms, this means that the challenges experienced among some Somalis in Finnish society are also attributed to Muslim students from other ethnic communities (Ubani 2018, 2019).

An overly simplified understanding of the diversity within Islam is also reflected in the ways of explaining the apparent differences in Muslim belief and behaviour by placing them along a single continuum, described in terms like religious/non-religious, radical/non-radical, conservative/liberal and extreme/non-extreme. For instance, the success of Islamic education teachers in developing trust with different families was explained by one principal in terms of him "not representing either of the extremes". The secular normativity imposed on Muslims, as well as poor knowledge of the existing variety in Islamic sensibilities, can also be seen in demands to "secularize Islam" in order to make it compatible with modern liberal society. As one principal put it, Islam "needs its Martin Luther", who would cut the "sharp edges" of that religion and help Muslims integrate into the West.

Furthermore, the lack of understanding of intra-religious diversity creates issues in practices of governance. The school principals' ways of outsourcing the management of religious diversity by letting a local imam or a single Muslim teacher decide what kinds of adjustments to the school culture need to be made in order to cater to the needs of "the Muslims" can be traced to understandings of Islam as a monolithic (and authority-bound) tradition. Principals' efforts to consult imams may be made in good will, but in actuality they can be experienced as an insult. For example, the reactions of Muslim parents to the cases where principals have asked imams to make statements on whether or not certain religious practices should be allowed in school have been strongly negative (Rissanen 2018). One Shia parent referred to a principal's move to consult a local Sunni imam as an experience of being stabbed in the back, and other parents who belonged to the community regarded the act as an indication that they were not considered intelligent enough to make their own decisions.

On the one hand, those Muslim parents who are regarded as well-integrated and moderate are continuously expected to answer questions, take stances "on behalf of Muslims", be experts of their religion, and be able to represent the other Muslim parents in the school. On the other hand, there were also principals who regarded "Muslims" as such a diverse category that it did not have any analytical value—and therefore could be ignored—while any differences among Muslims were treated as individual differences. Considering Islam as "too diverse to be talked about" can be combined with very stereotyping and generalizing views about it (Rissanen 2019). In a way, appealing to the diversity of Islam sometimes becomes an empty mantra, which is not based on adequate knowledge and instead used as an argument to justify the efforts of governance of Islam through the strategy of religion-blindness.

5   Protestant Conceptions of Religion and Culture

The third challenge of religious literacy that we have noticed is the naturalization of culture-bound conceptualisations of religion and culture, which indicates a lack of critical cultural self-awareness on the part of educational professionals. Previously, "neutral" and "objective" forms of religious education in the Nordic context have been demonstrated to be deeply influenced by cultural Protestantism but in a way that is not recognised by teachers themselves (Berglund 2014; Slotte 2011). Protestant conceptions of religion and culture also seem to impact the practices of governance of religious diversity in schools. In Finland, as a result of globalization and immigration during recent decades, there has been a shift away from the national narrative of a homogeneous Finnish culture. For instance, the national core curriculum seems to avoid essentialising language by describing Finnish culture as diverse in its essence (NCCBE 2014). However, the naturalization of Protestant conceptions of religion and culture is still prevalent in Finnish society. According to our observations, "Protestant bias" influences interpretations of religion and secularity in the school context, but this bias is rarely recognized.

The problem-centred discourse where Islam is seen as the main challenge for the social order of Finnish society is fostered by expectations that Islam should follow the same foreseeable logic as the Protestant tradition and its canonized doctrines; when it does not, Muslim families can be regarded as "difficult". Furthermore, religion-blind views of Protestantism *only* as a cultural tradition occasionally lead to disregarding the right of non-Christians not to be involved in what they feel is Christian practice. On an everyday level, this can mean, for instance, using the fact that a song is traditional as an argument to support the view that it is not religious. Moreover, statements that "we don't celebrate any religious holidays here" in schools where, for instance, Christmas is an important part of the school culture are good examples of the naturalization of Protestantism (Rissanen 2018, 2019; Ubani forthcoming).

The nature of conceptions of religion and culture can also be identified in the school personnel's perceptions of what are considered to be everyday life practices at school and their interpretation of guardians' and students' decisions. For instance, student participation in school festivities that are based on or have strong references to Christianity is sometimes debated. The end of autumn term traditionally includes a festivity with references to the birth of Jesus, be it in the form of songs, hymns or plays. What often happened in one of the schools studied is that the Muslim students participated in the rehearsals of the songs or plays but then were absent without notice from the school festivity when the presentation took place. In this situation, the teachers emphasised the way in which students do not ask for permission to be absent and the problems this causes when casting students in different roles, with the latter leading Muslim students to constantly be in lesser roles in various school celebrations. Absences without permission also occurred during swimming lessons and city hall receptions with dancing. Those explained as extra day absences due to Eid were interpreted by professionals more as a practical problem or the custom of a certain group in the community than a situation rooted in religious convictions or a sense of not having a voice to negotiate religious rights in school life (Ubani 2018). A "secular Protestant" mind-set also indicates a lack of recognition that religion is an important thing for some students; discourses on the incorporation of religious diversity and religious rights in school often reveal an agenda of "liberalizing students" from the religion-based demands of their parents and religious communities, revealing an underlying assumption that religion is not a significant identity factor for young people (Rissanen 2018).

The naturalization of Protestant or Christian elements relates also to the way in which professionals endeavour to promote tolerance through emphasising the similarities in all religions. In reality, however, views concerning the "common basis of all religions" may be based on looking at religion through a Christian lens. This was exemplified by one principal who quoted Jesus' words from the Bible ("let all the children come to me") to demonstrate that all religions promote the same positive values. However, only putting emphasis on the commonalities of religions and holding the view that other religions are in harmony with the core of Protestantism, since this tradition represents the "essence" of humanity, indicate a lack of religious literacy and can be seen as a form of cultural minimization and a religion-blind way of dealing with diversity (Rissanen 2019).

6 Conclusion

While discussions on the correct representation and treatment of religions as part of religious or intercultural education has been a much researched and discussed issue, resulting in Europe-wide recommendations for policy and practice (e.g. Jackson 2014; OSCE/ODIHR 2007), in this chapter our key argument has been that more attention needs to be paid to religion in the wider school culture, and that all educators—not only those teaching about religions—need religious literacy in order to be able to develop equal and impartial practices for the governance of religious diversity. In Finland, recent reports have adduced the inadequate adaptation of schools and teacher education to the changed demographics (Tainio and Kallioniemi 2019; Räsänen et al. 2018). We perceive schools and their personnel as official representatives of Finnish society for religious, ethnic and cultural minorities in particular, and the school essentially as a socialisation tool implementing state policies vis-à-vis its citizens (Windzio 2013; Weymann, 2010, 2013). For these reasons, the question of religious literacy of principals and teachers is an essential aspect to be highlighted when evaluating and developing the governance of religion policies of the Finnish state. In addition to intra-school culture, there is also a growing need and demand for connecting the school more closely to the surrounding community and communities (Jackson 2014); these aspects have also been recognised in the recent national core curricula in Finland (i.e. NCCBE 2014). In a post-secular context this seems to require a new kind of understanding and discernment regarding the global, societal, cultural, communal and individual aspects of religion (Ubani 2019), as has been pointed out by Dinham and Francis (2015) and Moore (2015).

Based on our case studies, we have detected certain key challenges in educators' religious literacy: these relate to perceptions concerning intra-religious diversity, the distinction between religion and culture, and Protestant conceptions of religion and culture. The case examples reveal education professionals' difficulties in recognising when religion is a relevant factor in the behaviour and interaction of different members of the school community—and when it is not. In other words, our examples depict both 'religionisation' and 'religion-blindness' as reflections of religious illiteracy. Examples of religionisation include attributing to religion some (negatively perceived) behaviours of members of a certain ethnic group, as well as not recognising features of the minority tradition as "cultural heritage" but instead as essentially religious. Examples of religion-blindness include moving certain behaviours beyond the realm of religious freedom by interpreting them as cultural, not recognising religion as a relevant identity factor of some of the students, holding religion-blind views of the majority religion as *only* a cultural tradition, and naturalizing culture-bound conceptualisations of the majority religion.

In other words, majority religion (Lutheranism) is often "culturalised" and minority religion (Islam) "religionised", with the exception that sometimes the behaviours or needs of religious minority members are "culturalised" in order to legitimize the view that declining to accommodate these needs does not insult anyone's religious rights. Thus, religionisation and religion-blindness sometimes appear as intentional strategies for legitimizing policies of everyday governance of religious diversity, but they also seem to originate from three areas where a deficit of religious literacy is evident: a lack of knowledge about the internal diversity of religions, problems in understanding the complex intersections of religion and culture, and a lack of cultural self-awareness. Thus, we argue that the advancement of education professionals' religious literacy in these three areas is needed in order to ensure that they are able to develop impartial practices of governance (Jackson 2014) that do not arouse feelings of exclusion among religious minorities; generally, in pre-service and in-service teacher education, attention should be paid to religious literacy as a vital component of educators' intercultural competence.

The development of "intercultural understanding" may be an insufficient approach when it comes to providing tools for handling religion in public schools today. As the examples presented in this chapter demonstrate, the reductionist treatment of religion as a form of cultural diversity does not advance religious literacy, and it may even lead to neglect of the specific challenges in encountering religious diversity and incorporating religious identities (see also Rissanen et al. 2016; Rissanen 2018). However, even though the education of teachers' and principals' competences to deal with religious diversity has for a long time lagged behind rapid changes in the social reality in Finland, recent years have witnessed several educational initiatives that focus on the development of educational professionals' intercultural competence and also recognise religious diversity as an essential topic to deal with (Räsänen et al. 2018). To support and fuel these initiatives, several research projects funded by the Ministry of Education are under way.

References

Barnes, L. Philip. (2006). The misrepresentation of religion in modern British (religious) education. *British Journal of Educational Studies, 54*(4), 395–411.

Bell, S., & Hindmoor, A. (2009). *Rethinking Governance: The centrality of the state in modern society*. Cambridge: Cambridge University Press.

Berglund, J. (2014). Swedish religion education: Objective but Marinated in Lutheran Protestantism? *Temenos–Nordic Journal of Comparative Religion, 49*(2), 165–184.

Berglund, J. (2017). Secular normativity and the religification of Muslims in Swedish public schooling. *Oxford Review of Education, 43*, 524–535.

Berry, Laura B., & Southwell., L. (2011). Developing intercultural understanding and skills: Models and approaches. *Intercultural Education, 22*, 453–466.

Biesta, G., Aldridge, D., Hannam, P., & Whittle, S. (2019). *Religious literacy: A Way forward for religious education? A report submitted to the Culham St Gabriel's Trust*. Brunel University London & Hampshire Inspection and Advisory Services. Retrieved November 27, 2019, from https://www.reonline.org.uk/wp-content/uploads/2019/07/Religious-Literacy-Biesta-Aldridge-Hannam-Whittle-June-2019.pdf.

Buchardt, M., Markkola, P., & Valtonen, H. (2013). Introduction: Education and the making of the Nordic welfare states. In M. Buchardt, P. Markkola, & H. Valtonen (Eds.), *Education, state and citizenship* (pp. 7–30). NordWel Studies in Historical Welfare State Research 4. Helsinki: Nordic Centre of Excellence NordWell.

Dinham, A., & Francis, M. (2015). Religious literacy: Contesting and idea and practice. In A. Dinham & M. Francis (Eds.), *Religious literacy in policy and practice* (pp. 3–26). Bristol: Policy Press.

Fagioli-Ndlovu, M. (2015). *Somalis in Europe.* Robert Schuman Centre for Advanced Studies. San Dominico di Fiesole, Italy: European University Institute.

Husu, J., & Toom, A. (2012). Finnish teachers as "Makers of many": Balancing between broad pedagogical freedom and responsibility. In H. Niemi, A. Kallioniemi, & A. Toom (Eds.), *Miracle of education: The principles and practices of teaching and learning in Finnish schools* (pp. 39–54). Rotterdam: Sense.

Jackson, R. (2014). *'Signposts': Policy and practice for teaching about religions and non-religious worldviews in intercultural education.* Strasbourg: Council of Europe Publishing.

Kuusisto, E., Tirri, K., & Rissanen, I. (2012). Finnish teachers' ethical sensitivity. *Education Research International, 2012.* http://dx.doi.org/10.1155/2012/351879

Migrant Integration Policy Index. (2015). Retrieved November 10, 2017, from http://www.mip ex.eu/.

Moore, D. L. (2015). Diminishing religious literacy: Methodological assumptions and analytical frameworks for promoting the public understanding of religion. In A. Dinham & M. Francis (Eds.), *Religious literacy in policy and practice* (pp. 27–38). Bristol: Policy Press.

Multiculturalism Policy Index. (2010). Retrieved November 10, 2017, from http://www.queensu. ca/mcp/.

Mundy, K. (2007). Global governance, educational change. *Comparative Education, 43*(3), 339–357.

Mäkelä, M.-L., Kalalahti, M., & Varjo, J. (2017). Monikulttuurinen suomalainen peruskoulu? Monikulttuurisuus peruskoulun opetussuunnitelmissa 1990–2010 luvuilla. *Kasvatus & Aika, 11*(4), 22–38.

National Core Curriculum for Basic Education 2004. (2004). Helsinki: Opetushallitus.

National Core Curriculum for Basic Education 2014. (2014). Opetushallitus, määräykset ja ohjeet, 96. Helsinki: Opetushallitus.

Nynäs, P., Illman, R., & Martikainen, T. (2015). Rethinking the place of religion in Finland. In P. Nynäs, R. Illman, & T. Martikainen (Eds.), *On the outskirts of 'the Church': Diversities, fluidities and new spaces of religion in Finland* (pp. 11–28). Zürich: Lit Verlag.

OSCE/ODIHR. (2007). *The Toledo guiding principles on teaching about religions and beliefs in public schools.* http://www.osce.org/item/28314.html

Poulter, S., Riitaoja, A.-L., & Kuusisto, A. (2016). Thinking multicultural education 'Otherwise'–From a secularist construction towards a plurality of epistemologies and worldviews. *Globalisation, Societies and Education, 14*(1), 68–86.

Revell, L. (2012). *Islam and education: The manipulation and misrepresentation of a religion.* Stoke on Trent: Trentham Books.

Rissanen, I. (2018). Negotiations on inclusive citizenship in a post-secular school: Perspectives of "cultural broker" Muslim parents and teachers in Finland and Sweden. *Scandinavian Journal of Educational Research, 64*(1), 135–150. https://doi.org/10.1080/00313831.2018.1514323.

Rissanen, I. (2019). School principals' diversity ideologies in fostering the inclusion of Muslims in Finnish and Swedish schools. *Race, Ethnicity and Education.* https://doi.org/10.1080/13613324. 2019.1599340.

Rissanen, I., Kuusisto, E., & Kuusisto, A. (2016). Developing teachers' intercultural sensitivity: Case study on a pilot course in Finnish teacher education. *Teaching and Teacher Education, 59,* 446–456.

Rissanen, I., Kuusisto, E., & Tirri, K. (2015). Finnish teachers' attitudes to Muslim students and Muslim student integration. *Journal for the Scientific Study of Religion, 54*(2), 277–290.

Rissanen, I., Ubani, M., & Poulter, S. (2019). Key issues of secularisation, pluralism and dialogue in Finnish public education. In M. Ubani, I. Rissanen, & S. Poulter (Eds.), *Contextualising dialogue, secularisation and pluralism: Religion in Finnish public education* (pp. 203–216). Münster: Waxmann.

Roy, O. (2010). *Holy ignorance: When religion and culture part ways.* London: Hurst & Company.
Räsänen, R., Jokikokko, K., & Lampinen, J. (2018). Kulttuuriseen moninaisuuteen liittyvä osaaminen perusopetuksessa. Kartoitus tutkimuksesta sekä opetushenkilöstön koulutuksesta ja osaamisen tuesta. Raportit ja selvitykset *2018*(6). Helsinki: Opetushallitus.
Sakaranaho, T. (2013). Religious education in Finland. *Temenos—Nordic Journal of Comparative Religion, 49*(2), 9–35.
Sakaranaho, T. (2018). Encountering religious diversity: Multilevel governance of Islamic education in Finland and Ireland. *Journal of Religious Education, 66*(2), 111–124.
Sakaranaho, T. (2019). The governance of religious education in Finland: a state-centric relational approach? In M. Ubani, I. Rissanen, & S. Poulter (Eds.), *Contextualising dialogue, secularisation and pluralism: Religion in Finnish public education* (pp. 17–37). Münster: Waxmann.
Sakaranaho, T., & Martikainen, T. (2015). The governance of Islam in Finland and Ireland. *Journal of Religion in Europe, 8*(1), 7–30.
Slotte, P. (2011). Securing freedom whilst enhancing competence: The "Knowledge about Christianity, religions and life stances" subject and the judgment of the European court of human rights. *Religion and Human Rights, 6,* 41–73.
Tainio, L., & Kallioniemi, A. (Eds.). (2019). *Koulujen monet kielet ja uskonnot. Selvitys vähemmistöäidinkielten ja-uskontojen sekä suomi ja ruotsi toisena kielenä-opetuksen tilanteesta eri koulutusasteilla. Valtioneuvoston selvitys- ja tutkimustoiminnan julkaisusarja 11/2019.* Helsinki: Valtioneuvosto.
Torfing, J. (2007). Introduction: democratic network governance. In M. Marcussen & J. Torfing (Eds.), *Democratic network governance in Europe* (pp. 1–22). Basingstoke: Palgrave Macmillan.
Ubani, M. (2012). Monoreligious education in a pluralist framework: The case of Jewish RE in Finland. *Religious Education Journal of Australia, 28*(2), 16–25.
Ubani, M. (2013). Threats and solutions: Religion and multiculturalism in educational policy. *Intercultural education, 24*(3), 195–210.
Ubani, M. (2015). Uskonto ja ryhmäidentiteetit koulun arjessa. In E. Hellqvist, M. Hietamäki & P. Pihkala (Eds.), *Uskonto ja identiteettipolitiikka,* (pp. 71–84). Helsinki: Suomalainen Teologinen Kirjallisuusseura.
Ubani, M. (2018). When teachers face religion in public education: Case examples from Finnish public education. *Journal of Religious Education, 66*(2), 139–150. https://doi.org/10.1007/s40 839-018-0064-x.
Ubani, M. (2019). Religion, multiculturalism and Finnish schools: the secularist-multiculturalist transition. In M. Ubani, I. Rissanen, & S. Poulter (Eds.), *Contextualising dialogue, secularisation and pluralism: Religion in Finnish public education* (pp. 105–126). Münster: Waxmann.
Ubani, M. (forthcoming). *Religion, multiculturalism and conflict in Finnish educational policy and practice.* Manuscript.
Ubani, M., & Ojala, E. (2018). Introduction. *Journal of Religious Education, 66*(2), 79–83. https://doi.org/10.1007/s40839-018-0067-7.
Varjonen, S., Nortio, E., Mähönen, T., & Jasinskaja-Lahti, I. (2017). Negotiations of immigrants' cultural citizenship in discussions among majority members and immigrants in Finland. *Qualitative Psychology, 5*(1), 85–98. https://doi.org/10.1037/qup0000074.
Vitikka, E., Krokfors, L., & Hurmerinta, E. (2012). The finnish national core curriculum: Structure and development. In H. Niemi, A. Toom, & A. Kallioniemi (Eds.), *Miracle of education* (pp. 83–96). Rotterdam: Sense.
Weymann, A. (2010). The educating state: Historical developments and current trends. In K. Martens, A.-K. Nagel, M. Windzio, & A. Weyman (Eds.), *Transformation of education policy* (pp. 53–73). Basingstoke: Palgrave Macmillan.
Weymann, A. (2013). Integration and the education state: Institutional history and public discourse in England, France, Germany, and the US. In M. Windzio (Ed.), *Integration and inequality in educational institutions* (pp. 21–41). Dordrecht, New York: Springer.

Windzio, M. (2013). Integration and inequality in educational institutions: An institutional perspective. In M. Windzio (Ed.), *Integration and inequality in educational institutions* (pp. 3–18). Dordrecht, New York: Springer.

Wright, A. (2004). *Religion, education and post-modernity*. London: Routledge Falmer.

Zilliacus, H., Paulsrud, B. A., & Holm, G. (2017). Essentializing vs. non-essentializing students' cultural identities: Curricular discourses in Finland and Sweden. *Journal of Multicultural Discourses, 12*(2), 166–180. https://doi.org/10.1080/17447143.2017.1311335.

Governing Divorce Practices of Somali Finnish Muslims: Does Religious Literacy Matter?

Mulki Al-Sharmani and Sanna Mustasaari

Abstract This chapter employs the concept of religious literacy to examine the divorce practices of Finnish Muslims of Somali background and the roles mosques play in issuing religious divorces. Drawing on field-based research, we argue that Finnish Somalis, in their divorce practices, make use of both Islamic and civil state laws, adopting non-binary approach towards both systems. We problematize the essentialist notion of Islamic family law that is posited in opposition to secular state codes, which one often finds in public debates on Islam and family law. We examine, furthermore, how women's unequal access to divorce (compared to men) in Islamic law works in the Finnish context. In relation to this, we shed light on the complexities of the role and authority of mosques in issuing religious divorces to women when their husbands do not consent. We note that women's agency and access to divorce are not merely determined by the legal systems but also by the intersecting structures of power relations and resources in their lives. We conclude with some final reflections on the relevance of the concept of religious literacy with regards to our findings.

Keywords Religious literacy · Islamic family law · Muslim divorce · Gender · Governance of Islam

1   Introduction

Research on Muslim marriage and divorce practices in Finland is recent (Al-Sharmani 2015, 2017; Al-Sharmani and Ismail 2017; Al-Sharmani et al. 2017; Mustasaari and Al-Sharmani 2018; Al-Sharmani 2019). The concept of religious literacy, in particular, has not yet been explored in investigating Muslim marriage and divorce practices in Finland or in the larger European context. In this chapter, our aim is to fill this gap. Focusing on Somali Muslims' divorce practices in Finland, we examine the relevance of the concept religious literacy to the understanding of Muslim family practices in Finland and the related issue of the governance of Islam in the country.

M. Al-Sharmani (✉) · S. Mustasaari
University of Helsinki, Helsinki, Finland
e-mail: mulki.al-sharmani@helsinki.fi

© The Author(s) 2020   55
T. Sakaranaho et al. (eds.), *The Challenges of Religious Literacy*,
SpringerBriefs in Religious Studies, https://doi.org/10.1007/978-3-030-47576-5_5

We use the concept religious literacy to shed light on the complex, dynamic and non-binary relationship of Islamic family law to relevant Finnish civil codes as demonstrated in the divorce practices of our interlocutors. Somali Finnish women and men often divorce (and marry) in ways that integrate the two legal systems rather than positing them in opposition to one another. We also highlight how the concept can be helpful in de-essentializing Islamic family law with regard to women's agency. Thus we show how Somali Muslim women's access to Islamic divorce is not necessarily or singularly impacted by the unequal divorce rights of women and men in Islamic legal tradition but rather by a combination of factors that differentiate women's access to family-based resources and knowledge of the two legal systems.

Our analysis is based on field research conducted as part of an Academy of Finland project (2013–2018), which investigated how Muslims in Finland organize marriage and divorce in transnational space and how the Finnish state understands and facilitates their wellbeing.[1] In particular, we draw on interview data collected from divorced women and men and from family dispute mediators in 5 mosques,[2] in the period from 2013 to 2016 as well as four year ethnographic research in one Helsinki mosque focusing on its program for family wellbeing (which includes mediation and adjudication work in divorce cases).[3] Our arguments are also informed by data collected by the authors of this chapter from interviews conducted in 2017 with leading religious actors in 8 mosques on their work in solemnization of marriages.

We structure the chapter as follows: The first section outlines how we understand and use the concept of religious literacy. The second section describes the Finnish context with regard to governance of religious minorities and in particular Muslim communities. We also outline the state policies governing marriage and divorce. The third section presents our analysis of the divorce practices of Somali Muslims in Finland, using the concept of religious literacy. We conclude with reflections on the relevance of religious literacy for scholarly and political debates about family law in Finland and in Europe.

---

[1] This project was titled 'Transnational Muslim Marriages in Finland: Wellbeing, Law, and Gender.' The first author was the lead researcher in the four year sub-study titled 'Transnational Somali Families in Finland: Discourses and Lived Realities of Marriage.' The second author was the post-doctoral researcher in the sub-study 'Governing Plurality: Marriage Practices and law.'.

[2] This research took place in the period from 2013 to 2017. The first author conducted semi-structured interviews with 5 divorced women and life story interviews with 5 additional divorced women. Post-doctoral researcher, Abdirashid Ismail conducted semi-structured interviews with 5 divorced men. We are also informed by related data collected from interviews with 16 married women and men (8 each), conducted by the first author and Abdirashid Ismail. The first author and Abdirashid Ismail also conducted interviews with members of family dispute resolution committees in 5 mosques in Helsinki.

[3] The first author conducted this ethnographic research in the course of four years, which consisted of participant observation as well as interviews with the mosque program organizers and participants.

2   Religious Literacy

One of the main functions of the concept of religious literacy as an analytical tool, according to Adam Dinham and Matthew Francis, is to critique the notion of religion as a problem, and to rethink the role of religion in the public sphere, arguing that the boundary between the secular and the religious is not given or fixed (Dinham and Francis 2015, 3).

Moore (2006, 2015) equally affirms the importance of understanding the ways in which religion is embedded in everyday life. Moore views religious literacy as the ability to "discern and analyze the fundamental intersections of religion and social/political/cultural life through multiple lenses." (Moore 2006, 1.)

The editors of this volume also put forward religious literacy as an important conceptual lens to avoid two serious analytical pitfalls, particularly in relation to governance of religious diversity. These pitfalls are: failing to recognize the relevance of religion and how to engage with it; or over-determining its role and significance in the lives of religious minorities.

We concur with the above-mentioned scholars. We contend religious literacy is not only limited to correctly understanding when and how religion plays a role in diverse social processes. It also goes beyond having adequate knowledge of relevant religion in a relevant context. Religious literacy, we argue, is also about acquiring an informed understanding about the often dynamic and processual relationship that members of a religious community have with their religious tradition. Hence, in this chapter, we use religious literacy not to reveal some inherent truth about Islamic family law, but rather to unpack and problematize essentializing notions about Muslim family norms and practices and show how Islamic family law interacts in dynamic and non-binary ways with the relevant Finnish civil codes, as our Somali Muslim interlocutors navigate both civil and religious divorce.

We also note how religious understandings may evolve as part of a process of re-engaging with one's religious tradition in a new context where multiple factors are at play. For instance, some mosques—in their roles as officially registered religious communities undertaking the responsibility of attending to the spiritual needs as well as the integration of Muslim families into the larger society—promote Muslim marriage and divorce practices that combine and reconcile between Islamic and Finnish laws. And some individuals also adopt new religious understandings whereby both Islamic family law and civil Finnish code have equal and connected role in regulating marriages and divorces. Moreover, these understandings are acquired through individual efforts to lead an Islamic ethical life (Al-Sharmani 2019). Such shifts in religious understandings can perhaps be understood as part of an internal process within the Somali Muslim community effort to reshape Islamic norms regarding marriage and divorce as they navigate life of a religious minority in the Finnish context and where Islam has recently been framed as 'a problem' (Martikainen 2014; Al-Sharmani 2015). This internal process is what the Dutch scholar Veit Bader calls 'internal religious governance.' (Bader 2007, 874.)

3   Multi-religious Finland and Governance of Muslim Marriages

In 1923, Finland issued its first Freedom of Religion Act. This law affirmed the equal right of individual citizens and communities to claim and practice their religion freely. Eighty years later with the issuing of the new Freedom of Religion Act of 2003, a new state discourse emerged that foregrounds 'positive religious freedom.' The country's new constitution, passed in 2000, also highlights the state's responsibility to support and strengthen the religious rights and identities of the diverse communities in the country (Kääriäinen 2011, 158).

Perhaps one effect of this new framework for governing religious pluralism in the case of Muslim communities has been that the number of mosques registered as religious communities increased from a handful in the early 1990s to over 50 in 2010 (Ketola et al. 2014). Accordingly, there has been more visible role for mosques in solemnizing Muslim marriages, mediating and adjudicating in divorce cases, and involvement with families in various activities targeting married couples, parents, and children (Al-Sharmani 2019). This does not mean that the work of mosques with families is solely motivated or enabled by these policies, but it does mean that these policies created legal and discursive space for the work of mosques in these aspects.

Marriage and divorce in Finland are regulated in the 1929 Marriage Act (234/1929). Historically, the state had no role in solemnizing marriages; this task belonged to Christian church alone. The situation changed as late as in the early 20th Century, and the 1929 Marriage Act gave all religious communities the right to solemnize marriages, with a permit granted by the government. For mosques, the right to solemnize marriage was particularly strengthened after they were able to register as religious communities according to the 2003 of Freedom of Religion Act, rather than registering as associations according to the 1989 Associations Act. In 2008, a law was passed to further regulate the solemnization of religious marriages (2008/571, after 1 January 2020, 1157/2019). The new law stipulates that mandate or license to solemnize marriages is granted to a person who is member in a registered religious community, provided that the registered religious community supports the permit. After the marriage ceremony, the marriage certificate must be taken to the local register office and inserted into the population register.[4]

Unlike marriage, legally recognized divorce belongs to the sole jurisdiction of the state. A divorce is issued by a district court upon a petition. No grounds for divorce are required, but there is an obligatory reconsideration period of 6 months, during which the divorce petition is kept pending. After the waiting period ends, the divorce is issued automatically if the spouses or one of them renews the application. If the spouses have lived separately for two years, the divorce is issued without a reconsideration period. Religious communities do not have the legal authority to issue state-recognized divorce, and the scope for private agreements about, for example,

---

[4]Contrary to some other European states, such as the UK, cases concerning disputes about the legal validity of religious marriages solemnized in Finland have not been reported in the courts (see for discussion, Mustasaari and Vora 2019).

arbitration or applicable law is very limited. Hence, for Muslims in Finland, it is often a case of legal pluralism where individuals use both Finnish and Islamic legal systems to organize their marriages and divorces. We elaborate this further in the following section.

4 Somali Muslim Divorce Practices

Somalis in Finland, for the most part, settled in the country since the late 1980s and onwards through refugee migration and subsequent family reunification, following the Somali Civil War of the late 1980s and early 1990s. With a total number of over 18,000, Somalis are the third largest migrant group in the country after the Russians and Estonians. They are also the largest Muslim community in the country where the total Muslim population is estimated around 100,000. This is a community that has been confronting a host of challenges such as low employment rate, low economic mobility, and racism (OSF 2013).

Somali women and men in Finland, predominantly, follow a two tier-system in their practices of concluding both marriage and divorce (Mustasaari and Al-Sharmani 2018). When marrying, some couples conclude the marriage at one of the licensed mosques, which then takes on the responsibility to do the paperwork needed to register the marriage at the local register office. Other couples have their marriage solemnized by an individual religious scholar, who may or may not be affiliated with licensed mosques. This usually takes place either in the family home or a rented party hall. Then the couples themselves take on the task of following the procedures for registering the marriage at the local register office.

In the case of divorce, couples also follow a two tier process. They conclude a civil divorce as well as Islamic one. There is no particular consequence that couples follow in concluding both divorces. In some of cases, for example, a wife would seek an Islamic divorce from her husband and the latter would agree to it. The husband would then pronounce the divorce in the presence of the wife and some of her family members, and then he would write a letter attesting to the conclusion of the divorce. Then the wife would initiate the civil divorce procedures. In other cases, the wife would initiate the civil divorce procedures and then would secure the Islamic divorce from the husband.

Most of our interlocutors see both Islamic and Finnish legal systems as important in their lives. Following Islamic legal rulings is viewed as an integral part of living a Muslim life and of being part of the Somali community in Finland. Abiding by the Finnish civil code is described as part of an effort to strengthen one's place in the society as a racialized citizen, and to facilitate the ability to claim certain citizenship rights such as family reunification in the case of marriage or the ability to officially remarry in the case of divorce.

Additionally, some of the interlocutors adopt a religious interpretation that advocate adherence to both legal systems in an integrated way as an ethical Muslim duty, rather than a practical necessity. This kind of religious understanding is being put forward by some of the mosques as well as increasingly being articulated by young educated women who are actively pursuing religious knowledge. (Al-Sharmani 2017; Al-Sharmani et al. 2017; Mustasaari and Al-Sharmani 2018; Al-Sharmani 2019.)

By using the concept of religious literacy to interpret the above-mentioned findings, firstly we can steer clear from a reductionist understanding that posits Islamic law in an oppositional relationship with Finnish civil code. Our interlocutors (whether individuals or mosques) are not approaching the two legal systems as totally separate but rather as belonging to one process through which couples navigated divorce. Secondly, one has to take into account the underlying social, historical, and policy-related factors shaping this approach. This is a context where many of the marrying and divorcing couples are immigrants or children of immigrants who do not have experience with codified Islamic family law. Instead, for the most part they organize their religious marriages and divorces drawing on uncodified juristic doctrines from Islamic legal tradition in fluid and decentralized ways. This, we put forward, may be facilitating their flexible non-binary approach towards both legal systems unlike a situation where couples have to engage with two state systems to secure both kinds of divorce. Thirdly, this is an immigrant community that has settled in Finland fairly recently and who is striving for inclusion and social mobility in the larger society where they confront racism, economic vulnerabilities, and to some extent Islamophobia. And, finally, this is taking place in a context where state policies promote and enable the participation of registered religious communities in the work of governance and creating social cohesion, particularly through the work of these communities with families (Al-Sharmani 2019).

When women need to secure Islamic divorce from unwilling husbands, civil divorce alone is not sufficient since women still need to severe the marital bond according to Islamic law. But how are women in such cases impacted by the unequal divorce rights in Islamic legal tradition which privilege men? In Islamic jurisprudence, men can sever the marital bond extra judicially through unilateral repudiation (*talāq*). The divorce becomes final with the end of a waiting period (*'idda*) that a woman observes after the pronouncement of the divorce, which is three menstrual cycles. Women, on the other hand can petition for judicial divorce (*tatlīq*) on specific fault-based grounds. Women can also initiate divorce (*khul'*) and secure it with the consent of the husband in exchange for giving up their dower and post-divorce financial dues (Ali 2006). Both parties can also reach a mutual agreement to divorce that entails a particular financial settlement (*ibrā*), often releasing the husband from some or all his financial obligations towards the wife.

This legal construction certainly makes men and women's access to divorce unequal in Islamic jurisprudence. To put in check the privileges granted to the husband, early Muslim jurists saddle him with hefty post-divorce financial dues owed to the wife particularly if she does not consent to the divorce or is not responsible for the martial rift. In contemporary Muslim majority countries, varying legal changes have been introduced to the codified family laws, which draw on Islamic jurisprudence, to restrict men's right to unilateral repudiation and to expand women's divorce rights (Tucker 2008; Welchman 2015). Nonetheless, many Muslim majority countries still uphold unequal divorce rights. This also applies to Somalis in Finland, who draw on uncodified Islamic juristic rulings to regulate their divorces.[5]

Our data, however, shows that it is not necessarily women and men's unequal divorce rights in Islamic law that primarily determine women's access to Islamic divorce. Rather it is a combination of factors that differentiates women's access to resources and knowledge, which in turn impacts their access to Islamic divorce. We elaborate on this point through the following example from our interview data:

Jamila,[6] a forty-two year old Finnish citizen of Somali background, was married for over a decade and was mother of three children when she decided to end her marriage. Jamila moved to Finland when she was in early twenties as the bride of a Finnish citizen of Somali background. The couple got married by an individual scholar in Somalia. They then concluded an official Islamic marriage in a notary office of an Eastern African country where they applied for family reunification visa for Jamila.

The marriage was not a happy one: Jamila's husband did not want her to be involved in managing their finances; was opposed to her wishes to pursue studies and work; and spent considerable amount of his salary on outings with his friends. When Jamila decided to get divorced, she knew she wanted to secure both a civil and Islamic divorce. Being a Finnish citizen with a life and children in Helsinki, securing a legally recognized divorce was an integral part of Jamila's efforts to start an autonomous life, and to be able to petition for child alimony. But securing the civil divorce was not enough. According to her religious beliefs, Jamila also believed that her marriage bond could only be fully severed with the securing of an Islamic divorce.

Jamila secured the civil divorce, but the Islamic one was challenging. Her husband refused to divorce her, and there were no family members to whom Jamila could resort and use their support as leverage to negotiate with the husband for divorce. Finally, Jamila decided to resort to one of the main mosques in Helsinki. The mosque family dispute committee called the husband and sought to meet with him to discuss his wife's petition for divorce. The husband was belligerent, rejecting the mosque's authority as a mediator and arbiter in the divorce dispute and even threatening the family dispute committee with violence. The mosque mediators repeatedly tried to reason with Jamila's husband. Few months later, the husband called Jamila and told her he did not want the mosque to be involved, to save his face in the community. In exchange for her withdrawing the divorce petition from the mosque committee, he divorced her by making the pronouncement in her presence and her neighbor, as well as writing a letter attesting to affecting the Islamic divorce.

---

[5]The majority of the interlocutors were married in Finland. The few marriages that took place in Somalia happened long after the Somali Civil War when the Somali Family Law of 1975 was no longer applicable with the collapse of the Barre regime.

[6]The names of the interlocutors quoted in this chapter are fictitious. Life story interview conducted by the first author in the period from 2014 to 2016.

Jamila's case reveals few noteworthy things. On the one hand, it illustrates the interconnectedness of the Islamic and Finnish civil codes in Somali divorce practices. Jamila could not consider herself divorced and move forward with her life without securing both divorces. On the other hand, her access to Islamic divorce was challenged partly because of men and women's unequal divorce rights in Islamic jurisprudence. But reading Jamila's case as a simple incongruence between Finnish and divorce laws would be misleading. Jamila's challenges also had to do with multiple factors that illustrate the need for a religious literacy that takes cognizance of the sociopolitical context in which her life was embedded.

It is a context where mosques as registered religious communities do not have the authority to issue legally binding Islamic divorce. In addition, it is a context where Jamila has no access to a court system where she can petition for Islamic judicial divorce. One could ask: do mosques need Finnish state authority to be recognized by members of their registered religious communities as having the authority to issue an Islamic divorce? The answer is not straightforward and points us to a number of underlying issues. It shows that what is religious law and how its authority is shaped and recognized is contextualized and layered. It also sheds light on the contestations around mosques as the moral actor fit to mediate and arbitrate in family disputes. On the one hand the model of Finnish governance of religious pluralism creates space for mosques to undertake this role notwithstanding their circumspect legal authority. On the other hand, the divorce (and marriage) practices of many Somalis also show that mosques are not always and necessarily the main body that undertakes the work of marriage and divorce conclusion. Many couples resort to a network of family relatives and individual religious scholars to navigate their divorces (as well as conclude their marriages). And there are couples who purposefully avoid resorting to mosques, particularly those run by members of their ethnic groups, motivated by saving face and maintaining a sense of privacy within their own local community. This partly may explain why Jamila's husband was persuaded to divorce her so as not to prolong dealing with the mosque, which is predominantly run by and attended by Somalis.

Our final point is that it would be also misleading to simply attribute the challenges that some women like Jamila encounter in accessing Islamic divorce, to men and women's unequal divorce rights in Islamic law. We need to adopt an intersectional approach that de-homogenizes Muslim women. Part of Jamila's difficulties in securing Islamic divorce also had to do with her weak family support. Her father, a religious scholar who lived in East Africa, was able to mediate between the couple frequently and successfully via transnational means of communications. However, when he passed away, she lost that support.

Perhaps it is fruitful to compare Jamila's case to another interlocutor, Deeqo[7] a thirty year old Somali woman who grew up in Finland. Deeqo moved to Finland when she was very young, attained high level of education, and was well-versed in Islamic religious knowledge. When Deeqo's marriage broke down and she decided to get an Islamic divorce, she encountered no difficulties, as she explained to the first

---

[7]Life story interviews conducted by the first author in the period from 2014 to 2016.

author. She explained that her family was supportive and were available for her as they lived in Finland. The husband, furthermore, could not afford to be belligerent and refuse the divorce, as Deeqo's family was fairly well-known and respected in the local community. Deeqo also emphasized that she knew her Islamic rights very well, and believed that her husband could not keep her in a marriage that she did not want. Deeqo's example shows us that her social resources, which were superior to Jamila's, enabled her to make religious-legal claims and interpret the law as being on her side. Accordingly, Deeqo and Jamila's encounters with Islamic law in a secular Finnish context were quite different.

5 Final Reflections on Religious Literacy and Governance of Islamic Family Law

In European debates, religious—especially Islamic—family laws or norms are often depicted as problem or exception to the norm of "secular" or "neutral" law (Bano 2017; Grillo 2015; Bredal 2018; Shah et al. 2014). In the Nordic context too, Islamic family law is increasingly represented as an "anomaly of secular society" (Bredal 2018; Mustasaari 2019; Mustasaari and Al-Sharmani 2018; Moors and Vroon-Najem 2019). The problem of this approach is that it depicts secularism as the normative ideal while failing to take into account the local historical particularities that define "secularism" in relation to (some form of) religion (Mahmood 2015) and in the process construct the distinction between private and public spheres. Accordingly, this approach denies that there is any relevance for religion in the public sphere and sees religion and religious norms as characteristic of the immigrant "other".

In May 2018, for example, the Finnish Minister of Justice Antti Häkkänen, who spoke in the ETNO-forum organized by the advisory board of Ethnic Relations, stated that while Finland is an open and diverse society, there is no room in it for Shariʻa Law. The Minister made the statement in the context of warning against a 'parallel society' where, for example, forced marriage and female genital mutilation take place and are condoned (YLE 2018). Such polarizing discourse seems to prevail despite the research-based evidence, which clearly points towards multidimensional and often mutually constitutive interrelationships of secular and religious law instead of an oppositional relationship of law and parallel legal systems (Bano 2017; Bredal 2018; Mustasaari and Al-Sharmani 2018).

These contemporary debates about Islamic family law whether in Finland or in the larger European context, in our view, are prime examples of religious illiteracy. Through adopting and repeating pathologizing assumptions and imagery of threat that Muslim family life allegedly embodies, religious illiteracy plays a key role in the process of legitimizing the marginalization of Muslims in European societies. Furthermore, as Melloni reminds us, similar to basic illiteracy, religious illiteracy can effectively be used as a tool of public policy not to extend political participation and civil development (Melloni 2019, 6). When in political speech Islamic law is framed as a key threat that Western societies are facing, it is not only Muslims that are being marginalized. Using promises of protection against the imaginary threat of Islamic law as bait in political campaigns is to use religious illiteracy to mislead the members of the public from debating issues that actually and urgently require social reforms.

Thus, religious literacy is useful in shedding light on the layered ways in which law (whether religious or secular) functions in the everyday life of Muslim immigrants. Our findings show that religion (in this case Islam) *matters* as a source of norms regulating Somali intimate relationships. Women and men (with the help of their families and mosques) draw on Islamic law to divorce even though religious divorce is not recognized by the Finnish legal system. However, Islamic law and Finnish civil laws are also interconnected in Somali divorce practices. Securing both Islamic and civil divorce are important for many and the determining factors are multidimensional. They include: Finnish model of religious governance, the history of Somali migration to the country, the migrants' living conditions and challenges as religious and racialized minorities struggling for empowering membership in the Finnish society.

Our findings also show the importance of intersectionality in understanding how law (religious and secular) is at play in individuals' life. It is not simply egalitarian Finnish divorce laws or gendered Islamic divorce laws that shape Somali Muslim women's divorce claims and practices. Rather it is how these women are differentially situated with regard to structures of power and their access to relevant resources such as family support, knowledge of both legal systems, access to effective mosque mediation and adjudication.

Finally, religious literacy also entails taking note of how immigrants' religious understandings evolve and develop. In our study, the practice of applying and reconciling both Islamic and Finnish legal systems in divorce practices goes beyond fulfilling individuals' pragmatic needs. For some interlocutors, it has become part of a new understanding of Islamic law and pious pursuit of an ethical Muslim life.

References

Ali, K. (2006). *Sexual ethics and islam: Feminist reflections on Qur'an, hadith, and Jurisprudence.* Oxford: OneWorld.

Al-Sharmani, M. (2015). Striving against the 'Nafs': Revisiting Somali Muslim spousal roles and rights in Finland. *Journal of Religion in Europe, 8,* 101–120.

Al-Sharmani, M. (2017). Divorce among transnational Finnish Somalis: Gender, religion, and agency. *Religion and Gender, 7*(1), 70–87.

Al-Sharmani, M. (2019). A mosque programme for the wellbeing of Muslim families. In M. Tiilikainen, M. Al-Sharmani, & S. Mustasaari (Eds.), *Wellbeing of transnational Muslim families: Marriage, law and gender* (pp. 59–77). London: Routledge.

Al-Sharmani, M., & Ismail, A. (2017). Marriage and transnational family life among Somali Migrants in Finland. *Migration Letters, 14*(1), 38–49.

Al-Sharmani, M., Mustasaari, S., & Ismail, A. (2017). Faith-based family dispute resolution in Finnish mosques: Unfolding roles and evolving practices. In S. Bano (Ed.), *Gender and justice in family law disputes: Women, mediation, and religious arbitration* (pp. 270–291). Waltham, MA, USA: Brandeis University Press.

Bader, V. (2007). The governance of Islam in Europe: The perils of modelling. *Journal of Ethnic and Migration Studies, 33*(6), 871–886.

Bano, S. (2017). Women, mediation, and religious arbitration: Thinking through gender and justice in family law disputes. In S. Bano (Ed.), *Gender and justice in family law disputes. Women, mediation, and religious arbitration* (pp. 1–21). Waltheim, MA: Brandeis University Press.

Bredal, A. (2018). Contesting the boundaries between civil and religious marriage: State and mosque discourse in pluralistic Norway. *Sociology of Islam, 6,* 297–315.

Dinham, A., & Francis, M. (2015). Religious literacy: Contesting an idea and practice. In A. Dinham & M. Francis (Eds.), *Religious literacy in policy and practice* (pp. 3–26). Bristol: Policy Press.

Grillo, R. (2015). *Muslim families, politics and the law: A legal industry in multicultural Britain.* London: Routledge.

Ketola, K., Martikainen, T., & Salomäki, H. (2014). New communities of worship: Continuities and mutations among religious organizations in Finland. *Social Compass, 61*(2), 153–171.

Kääriäinen, K. (2011). Religion and state in Finland. *Nordic Journal of Religion and Society, 24*(2), 155–171.

Mahmood, S. (2015). *Religious difference in a secular age: A minority report.* Princeton, NJ: Princeton University Press.

Martikainen, T. (2014). Muslim immigrants, public religion, and developments towards a post-secular Finnish welfare state. *Tidsskrift for Islamforskning, The Nordic Welfare State, 8*(1), 78–105.

Melloni, A. (2019). European religious illiteracy. The historical framework of a removed agenda. In A. Melloni, & F. Cadeddu (Eds.), *Religious literacy, law and history. Perspectives on European pluralist societies* (pp. 3–16). London: Routledge.

Moore, D. L. (2006). Overcoming religious illiteracy: A cultural studies approach. *World History Connected, 4*(1). Retrieved November 30, 2018, from http://worldhistoryconnected.press.illinois.edu/4.1/moore.html.

Moore, D. L. (2015). Diminishing religious literacy: Methodological assumptions and analytical frameworks for promoting the public understanding of religion. In A. Dinham & M. Francis (Eds.), *Religious literacy in policy and practice* (pp. 27–38). Bristol: Policy Press.

Moors, A., & Vroon-Najem, V. (2019). Converts, marriage, and the Dutch Nation-state: Contestations about Muslim women's well-being. In M. Tiilikainen, M. Al-Sharmani, & S. Mustasaari (Eds.), *Wellbeing of transnational Muslim families: Marriage, law and gender* (pp. 22–38). Studies in Migration and Diaspora. London: Routledge.

Mustasaari, S. (2019). Extra-judicial muslim divorces and family mediation in the Nordic Countries: What role is there for the welfare state? In K. Boele-Woelki (Ed.), *Plurality and diversity of family relations in Europe* (pp. 285–312). Cambridge: Intersentia.

Mustasaari, S., & Al-Sharmani, M. (2018). Between 'Official' and 'Unofficial': Discourses and practices of muslim marriage conclusion in Finland. *Oxford Journal of Law and Religion, 7*(3), 455–478. https://doi.org/10.1093/ojlr/rwy029.

Mustasaari, S., & Vora, V. (2019). Wellbeing, law and marriage: Recognition of Nikāh in multicultural Britain and the Finnish welfare state. In M. Tiilikainen, M. Al-Sharmani, & S. Mustasaari (Eds.), *Wellbeing of transnational Muslim families: Marriage, law and gender* (pp. 39–58). London: Routledge.

OSF. (2013). *Somalis in Helsinki.* New York and London: Open Society Foundations. Retrieved January 2, 2018, from https://www.opensocietyfoundations.org/sites/default/files/somalis-helsinki-20131121.pdf.

Shah, P., Foblets, M.-C., & Rohe, M. (Eds.). (2014). *Family, religion and law: Cultural encounters in Europe.* Farnham: Ashgate.

Tucker, J. (2008). *Women, family, and gender in Islamic law*. Cambridge: Cambridge University Press.

Welchman, L. (2015). *Qiwamah* and *Wilayah* as legal postulates in Muslim family laws. In Z. Mir-Hosseini, M. Al-Sharmani, & J. Rumminger (Eds.), *Men in charge? Rethinking authority in Muslim legal tradition* (pp. 132–159). Oxford: OneWorld.

YLE. (2018). Justice Minister: "No room in Finland for Sharia law". Retrieved December 19, 2019, from https://yle.fi/uutiset/osasto/news/justice_minister_no_room_in_finland_for_sharia_law/10218154. (22 May 2018).

Prevention of Violent Radicalization and Extremism in Finland: The Role of Religious Literacy

Marja Tiilikainen and Tarja Mankkinen

Abstract The chapter explores how authorities in Finland have dealt with religion, in particular Islam, on the policy level with respect to the prevention of violent radicalization and extremism. We understand religious literacy as a kind of sensitivity among the authorities to religion and religious communities, in particular when discussing and dealing with such complex phenomena. The chapter is based on the analysis of two national action plans for the prevention of violent extremism, in particular on how Islam and Muslims are addressed in these plans, including during their preparatory phase. In addition, we draw on the extensive experience of the second author with security-related issues at the Finnish Ministry of the Interior. Finnish authorities have been very careful not to frame violent radicalization as a phenomenon that would be linked to one religion or ideology only. They also promote participatory governance in order to bring partnerships with Muslims and other faith communities into governance structures and prevent violent radicalization. This participatory approach can be explained not only by sensitivity to religion, but also by some other contextual factors typical to Finland.

Keywords Religious literacy · Participatory governance · Islam · Muslims · Prevention of violent radicalization · Action plan · Finland

1 Introduction

The terrorist attack in New York in September 2001 was a turning point in the development of securitization policies in the West as well as in the activation and emergence of violent political movements both locally and globally. During the past fifteen years, terrorist groups have used Islam to justify the violence, and as a consequence, many Muslims and non-Muslims alike have suffered from the violence

M. Tiilikainen (✉)
Migration Institute of Finland, Turku, Finland
e-mail: marja.tiilikainen@migrationinstitute.fi

T. Mankkinen
Ministry of the Interior, Helsinki, Finland

© The Author(s) 2020
T. Sakaranaho et al. (eds.), *The Challenges of Religious Literacy*,
SpringerBriefs in Religious Studies, https://doi.org/10.1007/978-3-030-47576-5_6

of these groups. Moreover, violent far-right ideologies and movements in Europe have grown and become more visible. In addition to groups that base their ideology on the national-socialist ideology and ideas of race, the number of anti-immigrant and anti-Islam groups has increased. Therefore, life for the people who practice Islam has in many ways become difficult, as their religion is often seen as being synonymous with violence and, as a result, they face Islamophobia in their daily lives (e.g. Bayrakli and Hafez 2018). Since 9/11, a generation of young Muslims has grown to adulthood in a context where Islam is often seen as an enemy of the Western world and its values. At the same time, as religion has become part of the ideological and political battles and is actively being used as a tool to achieve different goals, the question of what kind of knowledge authorities should have on the role of religion in complex situations (see also Francis et al. 2015) and how they should consider freedom of religion in practice has become more important and sensitive than perhaps ever before.

The events of 9/11 escalated the global war on terror and the related development of securitization politics and counter-terrorism programmes aimed at increasing national security (Wæver 1995). In particular, Muslims in the "West" were framed as a threat or as "suspect communities" (Hickman et al. 2011), and their movements, connections and possible radicalization came under surveillance. According to Cesari (2012), as Muslims were constructed as an existential threat to the political community, it simultaneously justified exceptional measures of securitization. Moreover, security concerns in Europe resulted in a paradox involving, on the one hand, a desire to facilitate the integration of Muslims, and on the other, a perceived need to restrict the liberties of the Muslim populations (Cesari 2012, 437). Hence, authorities and civil servants need to make decisions regarding how to prevent violent radicalization and extremism, while at the same time there is a need to promote tolerant multicultural societies and nurture trusted relationships with stigmatized and securitized communities.

In this chapter, we will explore how authorities in Finland have dealt with religion, in particular with Islam, on the policy level with respect to the prevention of violent radicalization and extremism. We will utilize the concept of religious literacy (Dinham and Francis 2015), which we understand here as a kind of sensitivity among the authorities to religion and religious communities, in particular when discussing and dealing with such complex phenomena. In addition, religious literacy can be seen as an understanding of the larger contexts underlying violent radicalization and a willingness to ask more questions (see also Francis et al. 2015). Religious literacy entails an idea of having at least some knowledge about different religious traditions, but it primarily is a civic endeavour that supports the formation of a cohesive and inclusive society (Dinham and Jones 2010, 6).

In addition to a sensitivity to and awareness of religion, we are also interested in the participation of religious communities in the development of policies directed against violent radicalization. It has been noted that Muslims are increasingly included in the different sectors of governance, and partnerships are being built between civil society and the government (DeHanas et al. 2010). However, little reflection has taken place on the role and participation of Muslim communities in counter-radicalization and counter-terrorism activities (Spalek and Lambert 2008).

The chapter is based on an analysis of two existing national action plans for the prevention of violent extremism in Finland, in particular on how Islam and Muslims are addressed in these plans, including during their preparatory phase. In addition, we draw on the extensive experience of the second author with issues related to security and extremism at the Finnish Ministry of the Interior. It is important to keep in mind that the role of the second author has been instrumental in planning and writing the national action plans, and hence, the analysis can also be regarded as self-reflective to some extent. The first author has written the chapter as part of a research project "Young Muslims and Resilience", funded by Kone Foundation.

2 The Finnish Context

Finland has not remained outside the above-described European and global developments, even if the debates and policies related to security first emerged in Finland later than in many other European countries. One reason for this lag is that Finland, especially compared to other Western European countries, has remained population-wise quite homogenous. The change began at the beginning of the 1990s when immigration to Finland started to increase. At the same time, the number of Muslims also increased as many asylum seekers and refugees from majority Muslim countries in Africa and the Middle East migrated to Finland. The first notable group was Somalis fleeing the civil war in Somalia since 1990. They were not the first Muslims in Finland, however, as a small Tatar Muslim community has existed in the country for more than a hundred years—a Tatar mosque was built already in 1942. The Tatar community has maintained its religious and cultural traditions, but at the same time members of the community have become well-integrated with mainstream Finnish society, the community is small (approximately 1000 people) and the people generally remain quite invisible for the general public (Sakaranaho 2002). Another group of Muslims in Finland are those who have converted to the Islamic faith, but also they are small in number. Therefore, the public debate surrounding Islam in Finland has primarily focused on the fairly recent Muslim populations, most of whom often have a refugee background, in particular the Somalis, but since the 2010s also Iraqis and Afghanis. The estimated number of Muslims in the country is approximately 100,000 people, including the children of Muslim migrants.

The number of Finnish people who belong to the Evangelical Lutheran Church of Finland has been decreasing, but still almost 71% of the Finnish population were listed as members of the church in 2017 (Evl 2018). In general, religion in Finland is perceived as a private matter and the society is secular, but at the same time church is part of cultural family rituals, such as weddings, and it also has a role in many official events, such as the opening ceremonies of parliament. The first Freedom of Religion Act was passed in 1922. The rapid institutionalization of Islam in Finland since the 1990s has been driven by the need to become publically recognized and approved. In addition, migrant associations have played a central role in the implementation of various projects aimed at integration, and thus, they have been necessary partners for public administration officials (Martikainen 2014, 93–95).

The increasing presence and visibility of religious minority groups, Muslims in particular, in the public sphere and institutions has challenged Finnish authorities to consider how to strike a balance between already existing practices, on the one hand, and religious needs and rights on the other. The Finnish debates taking place along the "migrant integration–security nexus" have until quite recently mostly followed the developments elsewhere in Europe (Martikainen 2019, 32–33). The influx of asylum-seekers in 2015 sparked a vocal debate on possible security risks related to (mostly male) migrants, sexual violence, terrorism and support for militant jihadists in Syria.

The general attitudes of Finnish people towards Islam have been predominantly negative. For example, in a recent survey 62% of Finns—the highest score among the 15 Western European countries studied—responded that "Islam is fundamentally incompatible with [Finnish] culture and values" (Pew Research Centre 2018, 66). At the same time, Finnish authorities have considered collaboration with the Muslim communities to be of central importance, and they have supported the founding of representative Muslim organizations in Finland, in particular the Islamic Council of Finland (SINE) in 2007. SINE was funded by the government until 2014, when the funding was cut due to financial misreporting (see Martikainen 2019).

3   Preventing Violent Radicalization in Finland—The First Steps

Despite the fact that since WWII Finland had been almost entirely free of political violence of either international or domestic origin, the country started to gradually develop strategies to prevent violent radicalization, driven by EU-level counter-terrorism policies (Archer and Malkki 2012). The government of Finland has so far introduced three Internal Security Programmes (in 2004, 2008, 2012) aimed at enhancing security and safety broadly in different sectors of society. For example, the latest programme focuses on preventing and finding solutions to security concerns in everyday life, including homes, public spaces and work environments. In addition, "acts arising from extremist ideologies" are mentioned, along with school shootings (Ministry of the Interior 2012a, 55). School shootings have been a far more common concern for Finnish authorities than terrorism—the first incident regarded as a terrorist homicide or an attempted homicide under the terrorist law that came into force in 2003 only occurred in Finland as recently as August 2017, when a Moroccan asylum seeker killed two people and wounded several others in the city of Turku.

In 2012, the government of Finland adopted the first National Action Plan for the prevention of violent radicalization and extremism, and thus followed the steps of other Nordic countries. The title of the plan, "Towards a Cohesive Society", indicated its basic ideas: the plan and its measures targeted all forms of violent extremism existing in Finland, not only religiously motivated violent radicalization.

Until publication of the National Action Plan, knowledge about violent extremism and radicalization in Finnish society was quite limited. The Finnish Security Intelligence Service (SUPO) was the best-informed authority in this area, whereas the level of knowledge and awareness among local police was quite narrow. SUPO was responsible for counter-terrorism, whereas it was not entirely clear who was responsible for the prevention of violent extremism and radicalization—a task that was quite new at the time the first National Action Plan went into effect. According to the Action Plan, "effective, preventive action requires extensive collaboration among authorities and cooperation with civic society" (Ministry of the Interior 2012b, 20). At the same time, however, the Action Plan mostly focused on the work of authorities, leaving the role of non-governmental organizations and communities quite vague.

The National Action Plan describes the radicalization process only in general terms without making a distinction between different forms of violent extremism. Religiously motivated violent extremism is discussed in parallel with, for example, separatist extremist thinking and right/left-wing extremism. Moreover, possible challenges regarding religion and Islam are not specifically addressed. The Action Plan also highlighted the fact that violent radicalization is not a community-level problem, but rather an individual-level problem in Finland (Ministry of the Interior 2012b, 17). This can be regarded as a balanced approach, especially when taking into account the situation in 2012 during which time many other countries, such as Denmark, the Netherlands and the UK, were mainly focusing on radical Islamist extremism and terrorism. On the other hand, even the knowledge of experts about religion and its role in the radicalization process was limited and, in general, contacts with the religious communities were minimal.

One of the objectives of the Action Plan was to increase knowledge and information about violent extremist movements and ideologies among experts and the general public. The Action Plan also included information about the situation and preventive measures in other European Union member states and Nordic countries. One measure in the Action Plan was to publish a situation overview on violent extremism twice a year based on the information received from authorities. The report is an open document that describes the phenomenon and related developments in a comprehensive manner without providing details about individual people.

Another measure in the Action Plan was to hold regular roundtable discussions with the media. Topical themes related to the prevention of extremism have been discussed in these meetings, including such topics as whether media attention increase the popularity of and support for the violent extremist movements; travelling from Finland to the conflict zones in Syria and Iraq; what terminology should be used when talking about violent radicalization and extremism; and polarisation and violent radicalization. Hence, one of the aims of the Action Plan was to improve communication and collaboration between the authorities and the media, as well as to ensure that the media had enough background information on the complex topic.

All the main elements and issues that are still regarded as priorities with respect to the prevention of violent radicalization were already included in the first Action

Plan: the importance of cooperation, of trust in the democratic system, of including young people in the democratic processes, and of balanced communication. The concrete measures, however, were strongly led by the authorities and the role of non-governmental organizations as well as communities was limited. This situation developed differently in the next phase.

4 Moving Forward—The Second Action Plan

The second National Action Plan for the prevention of violent radicalization and extremism was prepared and adopted in 2016 (Ministry of the Interior 2016). This time, in addition to the authorities, representatives of select non-governmental organizations and communities were also involved in drafting the plan. In general, the level of awareness regarding the importance and sensitivity of religious issues had increased since the first Action Plan. There were several reasons for this change. First, knowledge about the complex role of religion in radicalization and extremist ideologies had increased (see also Francis et al. 2015). Second, based on the experiences with the first Action Plan, it was quite clear that non-governmental and religious organizations should be involved in drafting and implementing the plan. The third important reason was the cooperation agreement that was signed in December of 2014 between the Ministry of the Interior and Finn Church Aid. As part of the cooperation agreement, Finn Church Aid and the Ministry of the Interior organized a study visit to Washington and Minneapolis in the USA in spring 2015. The Finnish participants on the visit were imams, representatives of the Lutheran Church and Jewish community, and authorities from the Finnish Ministry of the Interior, Ministry of Economic Affairs and Employment, National Police Board, Helsinki City and the Helsinki Police Department as well as from the Finn Church Aid. Also, some young Muslims participated in the trip. The programme for the visit was comprehensive, including several meetings with representatives from religious communities in the USA. In addition, the discussions and interactions between the members of the group during the visit guided the future writing of the Action Plan.

Consequently, the second Action Plan was drafted in broad cooperation with authorities representing the government and municipalities, some religious and other organizations, and individual people, among others. Muslim communities also had the possibility to discuss the content of the plan and give their feedback. For example, the second author of this chapter visited different mosque communities and Muslim organizations and presented a draft of the Action Plan. The participants and communities had the chance to provide immediate feedback on the draft and also send their written comments afterwards. Like the first Action Plan, the second Action Plan also targeted all forms of violent extremism in Finland, not only religiously motivated radicalization (Ministry of the Interior 2016, 14). Therefore, the feedback from the Muslim communities was crucial in order to make sure that the Action Plan did not stigmatize the Muslims. This was an area where the knowledge and experience of the Muslim communities were needed. The Action Plan does not mention Islam per se;

instead, the plan refers to, for example, the conflict in Syria and Iraq and to people who have travelled from Finland to the combat zones (ibid., 13). Furthermore, not only mosques, but also churches and synagogues, are mentioned as religious communities that should be included in, for example, cultural and global education at schools and as places where students could visit to increase understanding and dialogue between different religious groups (ibid., 27).

In Finland, the role of religious communities in the prevention of violent extremism is regarded as highly important. According to the Action Plan: "Religious communities can strengthen people's participation, social interaction and spiritual life. They can mutually support each other and take action if religion is being hijacked as a justification for violence" (Ministry of the Interior 2016, 14). In addition, the Action Plan states the following regarding the capacity of the religious communities to prevent violent radicalization: "Religious communities are experts and credible actors in matters related to religious interpretation. Religious communities can support individuals and groups that counter the recruitment of violent factions. They also play an important role in strengthening the communities' resistance to violence-inducing propaganda. Working together, religious communities can act against violence and spread the message that violence can never be justified on the basis of religion" (ibid., 18).

Based on the Action Plan, certain measures in which religion and religious actors had a central role were initiated. For example, the *Reach Out* project (2016–2019) was launched by Finn Church Aid. The objective of the project was to establish a close-knit community uniting the authorities, organisations, various communities and religious actors to work together under the umbrella of preventing violent radicalization and extremism. As part of the project, the participants received intensive support for their efforts at curbing violent radicalization and extremism. These activities included, for example, seminars held in different parts of Finland involving authorities and representatives of Muslim communities. In addition, authorities were provided support in issues related to religion, and mothers whose children had been radicalized and travelled to/died in Syria were provided with support as well. The goal was to make everyone's expertise and experiences available and to spread the knowledge about available services and best practices in different municipalities and regions in Finland. From the authorities' point of view, an important result of the project was the increased cooperation between authorities and religious communities and, through this collaboration, increased awareness of the role of religion in violent radicalization. In addition, direct contacts with key persons in religious communities who might be consulted when needed were created.

In general, knowledge about world religions among Finnish authorities is limited, and therefore, there is a need for expertise regarding religious traditions, those of Islam and Judaism in particular: these religions are currently seen as priorities by authorities since Islam is used as a justification for violence at the same time as anti-Semitism is increasing. Jewish communities in general are well networked and they have efficiently advanced issues relevant for them in Finnish society, whereas Muslim communities are less organized and they have been more passive (apart from the Tatars) in relation to working with authorities and the state. At the same time, cooperation between the Lutheran Church and different authorities has a long history, and often even one based on law. For example, priests and pastoral care are available in prisons and hospitals. The diaconal work of the Lutheran church is well-integrated in the field of social work in Finland and provides multi-faceted practical help with various problems that people may have in life. In addition, the Church is invited to give statements when new laws and other issues are being prepared that will impact its activities and field of operations. Muslim communities do not automatically have this opportunity. In addition to the lack of representation and organization, one likely challenge to greater collaboration and interaction during the past years has been the fact that the Finnish authorities have primarily seen Muslim communities through the lens of terrorism and violent radicalization, and therefore, their interest has been more problem-orientated.

Another example of a measure where religious communities have an important role is the so-called *Shoulder to Shoulder* project, coordinated by Finn Church Aid, which aims to combat hate speech and the hate crimes experienced by religious communities. The aim of the action is to develop ways that religious communities can use to support each other when threatened or attacked. Different activities include, for example, holding joint events for different religious communities, staging peace walks, making joint statements and providing visible support to those communities that experience such a threat (e.g. cleaning graffiti off the walls of sacred buildings together). This measure aims to decrease mistrust and conflicts between different religious groups, such as Shia and Sunni Muslims as well as Jews and Muslims. Terrorist groups such as ISIL have capitalized on the tensions between Jewish and Muslim communities in their propaganda, and therefore, the kinds of inter-religious dialogues and activities that support mutual trust are considered important.

5   Finnish Policies Against Violent Radicalization: Lessons on Religious Literacy?

Based on our reading of the Action Plans for the prevention of violent radicalization and extremism in Finland, it can be observed that the authorities have been very careful in their choice of wording so as not to frame violent radicalization as a phenomenon that could be linked to one religion or ideology only. In fact, the word "Islam" is not mentioned in the documents at all. Sensitivity for not stigmatizing Muslim, or any other religious community, can be considered as a token of the increased level of religious literacy, but also as a necessary step towards engaging and collaborating with faith communities in the future for the common good.

The authorities have also made a conscious effort to engage religious communities in the planning of the second Action Plan as well as preventative work, which will likely be reflected in the final outcome. Throughout the process, the authorities have also signalled that religion is not regarded as a threat, but as an asset in such common efforts. One possible reason for this approach might be the long history of cooperation between the Lutheran Church and the authorities. This makes it perhaps easier also for other religious communities to cooperate with authorities, and vice versa. In addition, the neutrality of the Finnish state in relation to religious matters (Martikainen 2014) has probably helped the incorporation of religious communities in efforts at collaborating with the authorities. At the same time, however, it must be noted that many Muslims are relatively new to Finland and the community is hetero-geneous, and therefore not well-organized, which has an impact on the opportunities for Muslims to influence decisions that concern them. The small size of the country and possibilities for non-hierarchical communication with authorities in general, in addition to the general level of societal security and trust, are other contextual factors that facilitate collaboration between authorities and religious communities.

In Finland, collaboration between authorities and religious communities is even included as a strategic guideline in the new police strategy on preventive work (Ministry of the Interior 2018). Hence, Finnish authorities promote participatory governance (DeHanas et al. 2010, 6–7) in order to bring partnerships with Muslims and other faith communities into existing governance structures and to prevent violent radicalization. This is not the case in all EU countries, however, and there are also differences between the Nordic countries. For example, in Finland and in Sweden civil society organizations and religious communities are actively involved in national efforts to prevent violent extremism, whereas in Norway and in Denmark they are not given specific roles in the preventative strategies (Ramboll 2017).

The Nordic countries signed a cooperation agreement in January 2015 to exchange experiences and develop common methods for preventing violent radicalization. Cooperation in research is also included in the agreement. Because of this close cooperation, religious issues as well as collaboration between religious organizations and communities are also regularly discussed. In Denmark, however, the civil servants working in the ministries are advised to avoid contacts with religious communities, which means that they are not able to ask for advice from religious communities nor invite representatives from the communities to meetings or events. In the worst case scenario, this strategy may lead to the development of parallel societies and decrease the sense of belonging among some minorities. It may also convey a message that religions are a threat to the society.

In Finland cooperation across different sectors, and between ministries, researchers, professionals and civil society, seems to be easier and less hierarchical than in many other countries. One reason for this may be the relatively long history of associations (including migrant associations) working together with public author-ities through the implementation of various projects (Martikainen 2014). In addi-tion, social cohesion is still quite strong and societal trust high. According to the Eurobarometer (2017), the level of trust in public administration among the Finnish people (together with people from Luxembourg) was the highest in the EU (77% of the population). Ninety-four per cent of Finns reported that they trust the army (the highest score among the studied EU countries) and 91% the police. Studies among people with a migrant background in Finland show similar trends. According to one population study, people with a foreign background reported that they for the most part trust—even more than the native-born population—the social and health care services, the judicial system and the police: for example, 82.8% of them claimed they trust the police, whereas the respective number among the native-born Finnish population was 74.6% (Castaneda et al. 2015, 18−19).

In the European Union, efforts at preventing violent radicalization and extremism are continuously developing, and it is one of the top priorities in the area of justice and home affairs. In June 2018, the ministers adopted a proposal (European Union 2018) regarding the European Union's priorities in the area, including a proposal to develop related structures and mechanisms. The European Union's priorities in matters of policy also include recommendations regarding religious issues. One priority area has to do with prisons and probation, rehabilitation and reintegration, and one of the recommendations is to increase the exchange of experiences on how best to provide religious counselling in prisons and to provide guidelines on working with and training chaplains, particularly imams, for prison and probation settings.

Cooperation with religious communities is also supported by the European Union. In the priority area of local and multi-agency approaches, the recommendation is to identify good practices and guidance for local cooperation in the preventative work taking place between local agencies and non-governmental organizations, including faith communities. Another priority area is ideology and polarization, where the recommendation to the member states is to establish a joint overview of the different approaches and experiences and explore possible further actions in relations with religious leaders, communities and institutions, including the training of religious leaders, pluralism, faith-related dialogues, funding and the monitoring of religious institutions spreading a militant Islamist ideology.

Even though the level of knowledge regarding different religious traditions and groups among authorities who work at preventing violent radicalization and extremism in Finland is, in general, pretty low, the opportunity to collaborate with religious communities greatly helps them overcome any gaps in information and understanding. On the level of national strategies and action plans, such as the National Action Plan for the Prevention of Violent Radicalisation and Extremism (Ministry of the Interior 2016) and the new police strategy on preventative work (Ministry of the Interior 2018), this collaboration is encouraged and even obligatory. In addition, the wording and frameworks laid out in the action plans are important tools for authorities and grass-root level professionals and they will help pave the way for good practices and respectful and non-stigmatizing encounters, where both the rights and needs of the religious communities as well as concerns for national security may be approached and taken into account.

Regardless of the limited knowledge about world religions and religious traditions, Finnish authorities have been aware of the need to consider the role of religion in public sphere, in particular in supporting societal cohesion and preventing violent radicalization and extremism (see also Dinham and Jones 2010, 6). At the same time as it has been acknowledged that "religion matters", religion has been largely perceived as a collective phenomenon that has been approached through religious communities. Hence, less attention has been paid to understanding intra-religious diversity, which should also be recognized as part of religious literacy.

In this chapter, we have described the increased collaboration and partnerships with Muslim communities, in particular through the experiences and viewpoints of the authorities. In the future, research will need to reflect more the views of Muslim communities regarding participation in counter-radicalization activities (see Spalek and Lambert 2008). Listening to and assessing Muslim voices regarding participation and representation as well as the dynamics and possible tensions between different actors and power positions would be a needed step in developing the idea of religious literacy further and what it could practically mean in the prevention of violent radicalization and extremism.

References

Archer, T., & Malkki, L. (2012). Miten terrorismin ja radikalisoitumisen vastaisesta toiminnasta tuli tärkeä kysymys Suomessa? In T. Martikainen & M. Tiilikainen (Eds.), *Islam, hallinta ja turvallisuus* (pp. 79–107). Turku: Eetos.

Bayrakli, E., & Hafez, F. (Eds.). (2018). *European Islamophobia Report 2017*. Ankara, Istanbul, Washington D.C, Cairo: SETA.

Castaneda, A., Larja, L., Nieminen, T., Jokela, S., Suvisaari, J., Rask, S., et al. (2015). *Ulkomaalaistaustaisten psyykkinen hyvinvointi, turvallisuus ja osallisuus. Ulkomaista syntyperää olevien työ ja hyvinvointi -tutkimus 2014 (UTH)*. Helsinki: THL. Retrieved November 11, 2018, from http://www.julkari.fi/bitstream/handle/10024/127023/URN_ISBN_978-952-302-535-6.pdf?sequence=2.

Cesari, J. (2012). Securitization of Islam in Europe. *Die Welt des Islams, 52*(3/4), 430–449.

DeHanas, D. N., O'Toole, T., Modood, T., & Meer, N. (2010). Researching Muslim participation in contemporary governance: A brief introduction. *Muslim Participation in Contemporary Governance. Working Paper*, No. 1. Centre for the Study of Ethnicity and Citizenship, University of Bristol.

Dinham, A., & Francis, M. (2015). Religious literacy: Contesting an idea and practice. In A. Dinham & M. Francis (Eds.), *Religious literacy in policy and practice* (pp. 3–25). Bristol: Policy Press.

Dinham, A., & Jones, S. H. (2010). *Religious literacy leadership in higher education: An analysis of challenges of religious faith, and resources for meeting them, for university leaders*. York: Religious Literacy Leadership in Higher Education Programme.

Eurobarometer. (2017). *Standard eurobarometer 88*. Report. Public opinion in the European Union. Survey requested and co-ordinated by the European Commission, Directorate-General for Communication. European Union.

European Union. (2018). *High-level commission expert group on radicalisation (HLCEG-R)*. Final Report, 18 May 2018. Luxembourg: European Union. Retrieved December 21, 2018, from http://ec.europa.eu/transparency/regexpert/index.cfm?do=groupDetail.groupDetail&groupID=3552.

Evl. (2018). Seurakunnat tilastoivat työtään. Suomen evankelis-luterilainen kirkko. Retrieved November 9, 2018, from https://evl.fi/tietoa-kirkosta/tilastotietoa.

Francis, M., van Eck, A., & van Twist, D. (2015). Religious literacy, radicalization and extremism. In A. Dinham & M. Francis (Eds.), *Religious literacy in policy and practice* (pp. 113–134). Bristol: Policy Press.

Hickman, M. J., Thomas, L., Silvestri, S., & Nickels, H. (2011). *'Suspect Communities'? Counterterrorism policy, the press, and the impact on Irish and Muslim communities in Britain*. A Report for Policy Makers and the General Public. London Metropolitan University.

Martikainen, T. (2014). Muslim immigrants, public religion, and developments towards a post-secular Finnish welfare state. *Tidsskrift for Islamforskning, The Nordic Welfare State, 8*(1), 98–105.

Martikainen, T. (2019). The founding of the Islamic council of Finland. In T. Martikainen, J. Mapril, & A. Hussain Khan (Eds.), *Muslims at the margins of Europe. Finland, Greece, Ireland and Portugal* (pp. 27–44). Leiden: Brill.

Ministry of the Interior. (2012a). A safer tomorrow: Internal security programme. Ministry of the Interior publications 40/2012. Helsinki: Ministry of the Interior. Retrieved November 10, 2018, from http://julkaisut.valtioneuvosto.fi/bitstream/handle/10024/79479/sm_402012.pdf.

Ministry of the Interior. (2012b). Towards a cohesive society: Action plan to prevent violent extremism. Ministry of Interior publications 33/2012. Helsinki: Ministry of the Interior.

Ministry of the Interior. (2016). National action plan for the prevention of violent radicalisation and extremism. Ministry of the Interior publications 17/2016. Helsinki: Ministry of the Interior. Retrieved November 11, 2018, from http://julkaisut.valtioneuvosto.fi/bitstream/handle/10024/75040/Kansallinen_vakivalt_radikalisoituminen_eng_NETTI.pdf.

Ministry of the Interior. (2018). Enska. *Poliisin ennalta estävän työn strategia 2019–2023.* Helsinki: Sisäministeriö. Retrieved December 21, 2018, from https://valtioneuvosto.fi/artikkeli/-/asset_pub lisher/1410869/poliisin-uusi-strategia-siirtaa-painopistetta-ennaltaehkaisyyn.

Pew Research Center. (2018). Being Christian in Western Europe. Retrieved April 2, 2019, from https://www.pewforum.org/2018/05/29/being-christian-in-western-europe/.

Ramboll. (2017). Efforts to prevent extremism in the Nordic countries: Mapping. Denmark: Ramboll. Retrieved November 11, 2018, from http://uim.dk/publikationer/efforts-to-prevent-ext remism-in-the-nordic-countries.

Sakaranaho, T. (2002). Kansamme tuntematon väestönosa. Suomalaisten tataarimuslimien julk-isuuskuva. In T. Sakaranaho, & H. Pesonen (Eds.), *Uskonto, julkisuus ja muuttuva yhteiskunta* (pp. 132–159). Helsinki: Yliopistopaino.

Spalek, B., & Lambert, R. (2008). Muslim communities, counter-terrorism and counter-radicalisation: A critically reflective approach to engagement. *International Journal of Law, Crime and Justice, 36,* 257–270.

Wæver, O. (1995). Securitization and Desecuritization. In R. D. Lipschutz (Ed.), *On security* (pp. 46–86). New York: Columbia University Press.

Conclusions: Religious Literacy Promotes Absorptive Capacity, Inclusion and Reflexivity in Society

Timo Aarrevaara, Tuula Sakaranaho, and Johanna Konttori

Abstract In this book we have sought new perspectives for religious literacy by defining it as a governance function in society. This concluding chapter examines the frameworks for creating new knowledge and skills for actors in the civil service, in other service sectors and industry by considering the expositions of chapter authors elsewhere in the book. As noted variously by the authors, there is no unified scholarly debate on religious literacy, but there is a debate that should be recognised in Finnish society with its expanding pluralism by understanding how secular laws and religious practices intersect will be greatly improved as increased religious literacy develops in Finland. Religious literacy should be seen broadly within civil administration as a key factor in its performance.

Keywords Religious literacy · Governance · Civil service · Absorptive capacity

In this volume, the focal point is religious literacy and illiteracy in secular society, and the chapters have presented discussion on the theme of religious literacy in different contexts of the religious landscape, where the aspect of utilisation of religious debate is a common feature. In the civil service, the theme can be viewed as a performance factor. Requirements imposed on authorities' capacity for religious literacy increased during the 2010s. Religious literacy can be necessary general knowledge for an authority but managing the theme can also have practical meaning. Accountability, transparency and dynamism are key elements of governance, and we examine this phenomenon with the concepts of absorption, inclusion and reflexivity. Religious debates culminate in these modern characteristics of governance. To make these principles a useful tool for a relationship between the operating environment and the organisation, we have interpreted religious literacy as a contingency. This

T. Aarrevaara (✉)
University of Lapland, Rovaniemi, Finland
e-mail: timo.aarrevaara@ulapland.fi

T. Sakaranaho · J. Konttori
University of Helsinki, Helsinki, Finland

T. Sakaranaho et al. (eds.), *The Challenges of Religious Literacy*,
SpringerBriefs in Religious Studies, https://doi.org/10.1007/978-3-030-47576-5_7

contingency may be the effect of the operating environment on building an organisation or managing it, or finding ways to manage uncertainty (Aarrevaara et al. 2017).

1 Religious Literacy and Administrative Practices

Contingencies are effective and efficient features of organisations that support them to do the right things at the right time (Pfeffer and Salancik 2003). Contingencies can shape administrative practices in both loosely coupled religious communities and in tightly organised administrative organisations. Professionalism in administration is the ability to increase absorptive capacity, which refers to recognising and utilising external properties in the actions and work of the administration (Schmitt and Klaner 2015). This comes out well in Teemu Pauha's and Johanna Konttori's chapter on the mosque debate. According to them, it is not possible for an administration to pick one definition over others. They identified tensions between electoral candidates' commitment to religious freedom and their opposition to the proposed mosque. The authors also referred to the sociologist of religion Allievi's (2014) analysis on European debates about mosques. He has noted that the resistance to mosques can be roughly divided into two categories. On one hand, people are against mosque plans because of the tangible effects that mosques are supposed to have. These include the decline in property values, noise, increased traffic, and violent crime. On the other hand, some oppose mosques for cultural reasons, for example, because Islam is perceived as being incompatible with European values.

Religious literacy can contribute to the absorptive capacity of the administration to identify areas of activity in which the functions of civil administration are important. Absorptive capacity also means the ability to bring out essential religious themes, consistently deal with religious themes in stakeholder action, and the ability of authorities to bring religious issues into arguments in civil proceedings.

Another important feature of administration is inclusion as a characteristic of cognitive structures forming common perceptions. It can be seen as an ability to interpret and utilise the new knowledge and skills of administrators in understanding religious literacy. In this book, Marja Tiilikainen and Tarja Mankkinen present a relevant perspective on tackling strategic opportunities and actions to increase the capacity of governance. From this angle, reflexivity means capacity for strategic opportunities and increasing understanding of religious literacy in government. According to the authors, the typical feature of the administration is the tensions between existing administrative practices and religious needs, and they call this more precisely a migrant integration—security nexus. The result of this inclusion is an increase in capacity that can utilise religious literacy and increase the capacity of civil administration. By defining these contingencies, the administration can find solutions or operational practices for significant religious-based problems in administration (Hamann 2017).

The chapters in this book illustrate frameworks and practices that create the absorptive capacity to recognise religious literacy and use it in evidence-based decision making. There is a need to develop common perceptions that underpin the concept of inclusion as a means of understanding and interpreting religious literacy in the public administration, the third sector and industry.

Nykänen and Linjakumpu point out that religious and religion-related networks are embedded in secular institutions. These political and economic mechanisms have not yet been sufficiently studied in the scholarly literature. Based on the chapters in this book, religious literacy provides tools for government to operate in the framework of multicultural and multilevel governance. However, different solutions are offered in the chapters, depending on whether the aim is to influence tangible decisions as in a chapter on the mosque debate by Pauha and Konttori. Another angle is to enhance cultural diversity, as described elsewhere in this book by Al-Sharmani and Mustasaari in a chapter on governing divorce. The task of scholars is to produce research-based evidence for decision-making taking into account multidimensional secular and religious law.

For governments it is a challenge to create capacity in public administration for intra-religious diversity in practices of governance (Sakaranaho 2018, 2019). Based on experience from schools, Rissanen, Ubani and Sakaranaho have noted that governance is effective if it is based on interdependence and negotiation. The tools needed for better governance include more evaluation and development if governance policies relating to religion. Tiilikainen and Mankkinen point out that governments have tangible needs to wind partnerships with faith communities into existing governance structures. These include supporting people's personal choices as well as preventing violent radicalisation.

The third factor is reflectivity as an ability to predict future actions of civil administration. In the past few years, there has been a strong trend in Europe to boost the administration's ability to engage in societal interaction on key issues, and to draw conclusions from the dialogue about the future (Rask et al. 2018). Aini Linjakumpu and Tapio Nykänen found religiously-motivated practices and social networking. For them, religious literacy is a key skill that the administration needs to have to hold a debate on entrepreneurship as one of the major drivers of society and the economy. A credible administrative review of these themes means a consistent dialogue with ethics and environment. It is a large challenge that this dialogue has a common framework and concepts that make it possible to set common goals and conclusions for different groups in this debate. Without this dialogue, significant resources related to the religion cannot be identified and recognized.

The above-mentioned three areas of religious literacy in civil service are combined with the drive for dynamic control, which refers to the ability of policy making to handle issues in a rapidly changing environment requiring a continuous dialogue about policies regarding religious themes in society. In this framework, dynamic governance refers to dynamic interactions between key actors as an exploratory, inductive approach in setting performance standards for good governance.

2 Towards Conceptual Frameworks of Religious Literacy

Religious literacy is a unifying factor between the chapters of this book and serves as a conversation and framework for the meaning of religion in society. Thus, religious literacy does not constitute a unified scholarly debate, but rather a framework that can be interpreted by building capacity for governance, decision-making and social interaction. The aim of this summary is to bring out different contexts of religious literacy and find similarities and dissimilarities of understanding religious literacy. Here we also want to contribute to the debate concerning a useful conceptual framework of religious literacy in secular societies.

Our assumption in this book is that religious literacy is a pressing matter in all fields of a pluralistic society. The chapters confirm this view, but partly on different grounds. The chapter on Somali Finnish Divorce Practices by Mulki Al-Sharmani and Sanna Mustasaari, describes the approach of Islamic and Civic State Laws taking place in Finnish society governing religious pluralism. The chapter highlights the need to develop a religious literacy concept. Through this concept, actors in the divorce process can understand the factors that support the equal treatment of parties in administration and in the courts. Understanding the intersectionality of religious and secular laws can also provide enlightenment of the means by which it is possible for actors to be heard.

In this book, there is also criticism of the approach of interpreting religions as a special case. Religious identities, religious communities and individual believers choose some things from the religious basket and leave others behind. From a governance point of view, it is essential to identify the more important factors through religious literacy. The development of concepts and frameworks can enable authorities to identify essential problems and provide opportunities for discussion. From this perspective, religious literacy is social and civic competence in a pluralistic, welfare society.

The complexity of the religious questions in secular societies means that simply understanding the theme cannot provide guidance to the administration. Instead, the development of concepts and frameworks can enable authorities to identify the main problems and provide opportunities for discussion. From this perspective, religious literacy is needed in a social and welfare society. Multi-level governance means that religious communities can also become involved in individual solutions, social argumentation and decision-making.

The development of widely accepted concepts can be of decisive importance for trust-based and open-minded discussion between those involved in religion. It is largely about the themes that involve participation and discourse in decision-making and administration to promote the human capital of religious communities, and information and skilful actions in cooperation with the administration.

The chapters in the book deal with Finland, the civil administration of which has long been based on shared values. Finland makes an interesting reference country because multiculturalism has quickly become an important argument in society's decision-making and administration. In a chapter on religious literacy in education,

Inkeri Rissanen, Martin Ubani and Tuula Sakaranaho define the role of multiculturalism and religion at school. For the older rather than the younger generations, religion seems to be a difficult matter to cope with. For the authorities such as principals and teachers, the relationship between religion and culture has become more complex in the 2010s.

The chapters in this book indicate that there are new data and frameworks that can be used to find interpretations and solutions to difficult problems concerning social, cultural and religious diversity. Although the themes and data in the chapters are different, common concepts can be found for them. Religious literacy in this context appears to be an argument for the decentralization of administration in a multi-level governance framework. Multilevel governance also implies a strong consideration of cultures and religions as a resource and a tool for shared practices between religious communities and the administration.

References

Aarrevaara, T., Wikström, J., & Maassen, P. (2017). External stakeholders and internal practices in departments of teacher education at European Universities. *Higher Education Quarterly, 71*(3), 251–262.

Allievi, S. (2014). *Mosques in Western Europe.* Oxford Islamic Studies Online. Retrieved March 16, 2019, from http://www.stefanoallievi.it/2014/07/mosques-in-western-europe/.

Hamann, P. Maik. (2017). Towards a contingency theory of corporate planning–A systematic literature review. *Management Review Quarterly, 67,* 227–289.

Pfeffer, J., & Salancik, G. R. (2003). *The external control of organizations: A resource dependence perspective.* Stanford, California: Stanford Business Books.

Rask, M., Mačiukaitė-Žvinienė, S., Taugiene, L., Dikcius, V., Matschoss, K., Aarrevaara, T., et al. (2018). *Public participation, science and society-tools for dynamic and responsible governance of research and innovation.* London and New York: Routledge.

Sakaranaho, T. (2018). Encountering religious diversity: Multilevel governance of Islamic education in Finland and Ireland. *Journal of Religious Education, 66*(2), 111–124.

Sakaranaho, T. (2019). The governance of religious education in Finland: A state-centric relational approach? In M. Ubani, I. Rissanen, & S. Poulter (Eds.), *Contextualising dialogue, secularisation and pluralism: Religion in Finnish public education* (pp. 17–37). Münster: Waxmann.

Schmitt, A., & Klaner, P. (2015). From snapshot to continuity-A dynamic model of organizational adaptation to environmental changes. *Scandinavian Journal of Management, 31,* 3–13.